剑桥KET考试
口语通关周计划

金利 / 编著

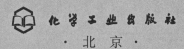

化学工业出版社

·北京·

图书在版编目（CIP）数据

剑桥KET考试口语通关周计划 / 金利编著. —北京：
化学工业出版社，2024.6
（剑桥KET考试通关周计划）
ISBN 978-7-122-45326-6

Ⅰ.①剑⋯ Ⅱ.①金⋯ Ⅲ.①英语水平考试–口语–
自学参考资料 Ⅳ.①H310.41

中国国家版本馆CIP数据核字（2024）第065048号

责任编辑：马小桐 马 骄 　　　　　装帧设计：张 辉
责任校对：王鹏飞 　　　　　　　　　版式设计：梧桐影

出版发行：化学工业出版社
　　　　　（北京市东城区青年湖南街13号 邮政编码100011）
印 　装：河北京平诚乾印刷有限公司
787mm×1092mm　1/16　印张9½　字数168千字
2024年6月北京第1版第1次印刷

购书咨询：010-64518888 　　　　　售后服务：010-64518899
网 　 址：http://www.cip.com.cn
凡购买本书，如有缺损质量问题，本社销售中心负责调换。

定 　 价：49.90元 　　　　　　　　　版权所有 　违者必究

前言

《剑桥KET考试口语通关周计划》一书写给正在备考剑桥A2 Key(KET)口语考试的考生。我们深知准备口语考试需要一定的时间规划、思路点拨、考点锦囊以及充分练习。因此，本书采用了讲解与规划相结合的学习方法，将这些要素有机地结合在一起，帮助考生顺利通关。

⏱ KET口语考试通关 = **合理的时间规划 + 思路点拨 + 考点锦囊 + 每周一练**

★ **8周学习规划**

按周规划好学习内容，跟着规划学，易坚持，更高效。

本书学习内容以周为单位，从考试内容入手，为考生规划好要学习或练习的内容，跟着规划走，利用碎片化时间来学习，用时少，效率高。

◇ 【周目标】每周开启学习前，了解本周学习目标。

◇ 【周中学】每周周中学习考试核心备考知识，掌握答题思路，积累考试词句。

◇ 【周末练】周六周日，集中演练本周所学。

一周内容，以目标为导向，学练结合，知识掌握更加扎实。

★ **思路点拨 + 考点锦囊**

考题呈现，剖析答题思路，分享KET口语锦囊，答题更容易。

在每周学习中，针对口语考试中的必考题型，本书给出了答题思路以及考点锦囊。同时，本书还包含KET口语考试的30个常考主题并给出与主题相关的"考官-考生"问答句型和答题关键词，为考生提供答题的资料库。

本书旨在帮助考生建立答题思维，而非死记硬背，有思路，有方法，有词句积累，考场答题更从容。

★ 每周一练 + 全真模拟

多样化题型操练本周所学，学后巩固练习，知识掌握更加扎实。

本书的练习题包括各种多样化的口语题型，如听音选择合适答语、连线、判断句子正误、模拟演练，内容涉及个人介绍、描述图片、讨论观点、日常习惯等，多维度操练本周所学内容，进一步夯实所学，打好基础，帮助考生有效备考。

通过每周一练和全真模拟题，考生将能够熟悉各种考试题型，锻炼口语表达能力，并在实践中提高应对考试的信心。

总之，本书致力于为考生提供全面而高效的学习资源，让考生在备考剑桥A2 Key(KET)口语考试时更有信心、更具备竞争力。希望通过本书的学习，考生能够顺利通过考试，实现自己的考试目标。

目录

熟悉考试

第1周目标

学习模块	时间	主题	
熟悉考试	Day 1	考试题型及注意事项	☐
	Day 2	考试流程	☐
	Day 3	评分标准	☐
	Day 4	常考话题及问题类型	☐
	Day 5	口语必备技能	☐
	Weekend	每周一练	☐

Day 1 考试题型及注意事项

在备考过程中，理解考试题型是非常重要的一步。A2 Key口语考试包含两部分：Part 1和Part 2。下面是Part 1和Part 2的考试内容。

部分		考查能力
Part 1	日常对话	介绍个人信息、阐述基本事实和简单互动交流的能力
Part 2	协作讨论题	语言组织和互动交际能力

部分		考查内容	具体内容
Part 1	Phase 1	通常是关于yourself "你自己"	考官会提问与考生个人信息相关的问题，包括姓名、年龄、国籍和学校等
	Phase 2		考官就学生熟悉的话题，如读书、食物、爱好等进行提问
Part 2	Phase 1	给出关于某一话题的5张图	考生之间讨论5张图片内容 考官就该话题进行提问
	Phase 2	主要谈论 "喜欢" 或 "不喜欢"	考官就该话题进行拓展提问

下面是口语Part 1和Part 2的考试要求及官方备考建议。

部分	考试要求
Part 1	考官询问关于考生个人信息和一些与日常生活相关的事实性问题；之后考官会用"告诉我一些关于……的事情"引出一个更长的问题
Part 2	考官说出具体题目并给予题目图片，两位考生根据图片和题目要求进行讨论；然后考官就该主题进行提问

关于Part 1，官方备考建议：

1. 考生在口语考试开始时感到紧张是很正常的。此部分使用的是简单的日常用语，目的是帮助考生进入考试状态。

2. 考生应该仔细听问题并给出相关答案。

3. 考生应该避免用一个词回答问题，要试图扩展答案，尽可能给出原因和例子。不过，在这个阶段，考生的回答不要过长。

4. 如果考生理解问题有难度，可请考官重复一遍。

关于Part 2，官方备考建议：

1. 考生应该仔细观察图片，并确认每张图片中的活动、地方或事物。

2. 考生应主要谈论所有活动、事物或地方，表达喜好及原因。

3. 考生被鼓励通过详细阐述自己的答案和回应对方的话语来尽可能延长自己的表述，例如，针对搭档的主意给出建议，或问一个问题使对话继续下去。

4. 话题可能包含与日常生活、学校、休闲活动、交通、城镇和城市以及假期相关的活动和地方。

口语考试答题注意事项	
Part 1	Part 2
1. 考生应该仔细听问题并给出相关答案	1. 考生应该仔细观察图片提示，并确认每张图片中的活动、地方或事物
2. 考生应该避免用一个词回答问题，要试图扩展答案，尽可能给出原因和例子；不过，在这个阶段，考生的回答不要过长	2. 考生应主要谈论所有活动、事物或地方，表达喜好及原因
3. 如果考生理解问题有难度，可请考官重复一遍	3. 考生可以通过详细阐述自己的答案和回应对方的话语来尽可能延长自己的表述，例如，针对搭档的表达给出建议，或问一个问题使对话继续下去

续表

口语考试答题注意事项	
Part 1	Part 2
4. 口齿清晰，确保两位考官都能听到	4. 仔细倾听你的搭档，准备好向他们提问以开始讨论
5. 充分利用作答时间来展示你的语言技能	5. 尽力回答问题。如果你什么都不说，考官将无法为你打分。犯了错也没有关系，和搭档及主考官进行交流才是重点

Day 2　考试流程

口语考试时长8~10分钟，Part 1考试时长3~4分钟，Part 2考试时长5~6分钟。在Part 1中，考生需要回答考官的提问，在Part 2中，考生要与另一名考生讨论，还要回答考官提问。

部分	时间	交流	任务类型	考生要做什么
Part 1	3~4分钟	考官→考生	考官依次向考生提问	回答问题，提供事实或个人信息
Part 2	5~6分钟	考生↔考生 考官→考生	根据图片提示展开讨论	考生讨论喜好并给出理由

Part 1 考试流程

Part 1考试流程	提示
1. 在备考教室准备考试	保持安静
2. 进入考场	带着评分表
3. 考官收评分表	听到Can I have your mark sheets, please? 这个问题时，把评分表交到考官手里
4. 考官自我介绍	通常为两名考官，一名考官提问，一名考官记录
5. 询问考生基础信息问题	对两名考生分别提4个问题，问题与考生基本信息相关
6. 谈论2个话题	2个话题会涉及10个问题，每位考生回答5个问题

Part 1部分，考官会轮流问考生A和B有关个人信息和日常生活的问题，时长3~4分钟。

★ 询问考生基础信息问题

考官会对两名考生分别提4个问题，问题与考生基本信息相关，比如，名字是什么、年龄多大、来自哪里、住在哪里等。其中名字为必问问题，其他问题随机。

★ 谈论2个话题

考官会谈论2个考生熟悉的话题，比如family（家庭）、hobbies（爱好）、school（学校）、weather（天气）等。2个话题会涉及10个问题，每位考生回答5个问题。

第一个话题，考官会先问考生A2个问题，然后再问考生B2个问题，最后问考生A一个拓展问题（Please tell me something...）。

第二个话题，考官会先问考生B2个问题，然后再问考生A2个问题，最后问考生B一个拓展问题（Please tell me something...）。

Part 2 考试流程

Part 2考试流程	具体内容
1. 发小册子	上面有同一主题的五张图片
2. 考生与考生对话	每一张图片都要讨论到
	Do you like...? 谈论喜欢/ 不喜欢并说出原因
	1~2分钟
3. 收小册子前的考官问答	Do you think... is...?/ Which of these... do you like best? 表明自己观点并说出理由
	最多2分钟
4. 考官收走小册子	
5. 收小册子后的考官问答	考官问基于图片的2个拓展问题
	考生分别作答
	最多2分钟
6. 口语考试结束	

Part 2部分，两名考生之间需要围绕几张图片进行对话，然后回答考官提问。其中涉及谈论喜欢/ 不喜欢、同意/ 不同意，以及陈述理由。Part 2考试时长为5~6分钟。

★ 考生与考生对话

Part 2开始时，考官会给考生一个小册子，上面是关于一个主题的五张图片，主题可能是"爱好""运动"等。考生需要根据图片谈论"喜欢/ 不喜欢"，每一张图片都要讨论到。回答问题时要说出喜欢/ 不喜欢的原因。

★ 收小册子前的考官问答

考生与考生对话时，考官会仔细聆听，并把控时间。几轮问答后，考官会分别询问两名考生1～3个不同的问题（通常是2个问题），问题形式为Do you think XX is X?（XX为图片内容，比如playing basketball, dancing；X为形容词，比如interesting, boring）。考生作答时，不仅要表明自己观点，还要说出理由。

然后，考官会分别问考生1个问题：Which of these XXX do you like best?（XXX为几张图片的主题，比如sports, hobbies）。考生作答时，需要说出最喜欢（图片中）哪一个，以及为什么。

★ 收小册子后的考官问答

收走小册子后，考官会基于图片问两个拓展问题，考生需要分别作答。

Day 3　评分标准

A2 Key口语考试的评分标准共有四项，分别为整体成绩、语法和词汇、发音、互动沟通。

具体评分标准如下。

分数	评分标准
5	能应对日常情景中的交流，中间偶有迟疑 能组织较长的语句，但除了事先准备好的部分，不能使用复杂的语言表达
4	完成情况在级别3和级别5之间
3	在非常熟悉的日常情境中传达基本意思 语句往往很短——只有单词或短语——经常出现迟疑和停顿
2	完成情况在级别1和级别3之间
1	即使在非常熟悉的日常情境中，也很难表达基本意思 回答仅限于简短的短语或零散的单词，经常出现迟疑和停顿
0	完成情况在级别1之下

分数	语法和词汇	发音	互动沟通
5	很好地掌握了简单的语法结构 在讨论日常话题时能使用一系列恰当的词语	大体是可理解的，并在话语和词汇层面上对语音特征有一定的控制	保持简单的交流 只需要很少的提示和帮助

续表

分数	语法和词汇	发音	互动沟通
4	完成情况在级别3和级别5之间		
3	基本掌握简单语法结构 在讨论日常话题时能使用恰当的词汇	尽管语音特征掌握程度有限，但基本上是可理解的	尽管有一些困难，但仍能保持简单的交流 需要提示和帮忙
2	完成情况在级别1和级别3之间		
1	仅掌握了几种有限的语法结构 说出的单词和短语散不成句	语音特征掌握程度非常有限，且表述难理解	保持简单的交流有相当大的困难 需要额外的提示和帮助
0	完成情况在级别1之下		

从上述评分标准中，我们可以看出，如果想在口语考试中得高分，需要做到以下几点。

1. 能够用英语就日常话题（详情见"Day 4 常考话题及问题类型"）进行简单对话。

2. 能够说出完整的句子，而不是只说一两个单词。（详情见"Day 4 常考话题及问题类型"）

3. 能够熟练使用如简单句、时态、连接词等基础语法。（详情见"Day 5 口语必备技能"）

4. 能够正确使用恰当的词汇。

5. 能够准确把握如重音等语音语调。

6. 能够发音清晰让对方听懂自己的话。

语音语调		
知识点	内容	举个例子
语速	语速自然，说话不快也不慢	
发音	◆ 熟悉48个国际音标，知道单词的正确发音 （详情见"附录 国际音标和单词的发音"）	like /laɪk/ 喜欢 cat /kæt/ 猫
重读	◆ 单词重读是指强调音节，一般会在单词的音标中标注出来	beautiful /ˈbjuːtɪfl/ 美丽的 important /ɪmˈpɔːtnt/ 重要的
	◆ 重读强调句子意思的单词，或者说话者想特意强调的部分	I love my new toy. 我喜欢我的新玩具。
弱读	◆ 句子中的弱读出现在句子中的虚词上，包括非实义动词、冠词、连词、介词等	I can /kən/ speak a little French. 我会说一点法语。

语音语调		
知识点	内容	举个例子
缩略语的读音	◆ 口语考试中常见的缩略词有： it's=it is　　　　　　　I'm=I am he's=he is　　　　　　　I'd=I would that's=that is　　　　　　what's= what is don't=do not	it's /ɪts/　　　　I'm /aɪm/ he's /hiːz/　　　I'd /aɪd/ that's /ðæts/　　what's /wɒts/ don't /dəʊnt/
语调	◆ 语调，即说话的腔调，指在说话或朗读时声调的抑扬 ◆ 英语有五种基本语调：升调（↗）、降调（↘）、升降调（∧）、降升调（∨）以及平调（→） ◆ 升调：常用于一般疑问句、列举事物等 ◆ 降调：用于陈述句、特殊疑问句、祈使句、感叹句等	I think so↘. 我认为是这样的 I like running↗, swimming↗, and skating↘. 我喜欢跑步、游泳和滑冰。

Day 4　常考话题及问题类型

一、熟悉常考的话题

A2 Key口语考的是考生熟悉的话题有6类，分别为个人信息、日常生活、假期娱乐、人物介绍、休闲活动和方位地点，共30个小话题。

日常话题					
个人信息	问候	日常生活	食物	假期娱乐	假期
	姓名		语言		交通
	年龄		天气		购物
	来自哪里		学校		网络
	家和家人		服装		音乐
人物介绍	人物描述	休闲活动	影视节目	方位地点	房屋住宿
	家庭生活		动物宠物		购物场所
	兴趣爱好		传统节日		用餐场所
	体育运动		科学技术		城市去处
	社会交往		生活常识		地方建筑

二、熟悉常考的问题类型

A2 Key口语常考的问题类型共有11类，分别为是非类（yes/no）、人员类（who）、喜好类（what）、时间类（when/which time）、地点类（where）、方式类（how）、频率类（how often）、数量类（how many/how much）、事实选择类（which）、描述类（please tell me）、二选一类（or）。

常考的问题类型		
问题类型	特点	答题技巧
yes/no 是非类	◆ 一般疑问句 ◆ 以Do...?/ Is...?/ Can...?等开头	1. 不能只说yes或no 2. 要用完整的句子进行补充
who 人员类	◆ who意为"谁" ◆ 通常会问"家里谁做某事、最喜欢的老师是谁、最好的朋友是谁"等	回答时，用完整的句子，不要只说人名
what 喜好类	◆ what意为"什么" ◆ 通常会问"最喜欢的学科、音乐、运动、爱好、颜色、食物"等	回答时，注意听what后面的名词是什么，比如music（音乐）、subject（学科）、food（食物）等
when/which time 时间类	◆ when/which time意为"何时" ◆ 询问时间	1. 答语常用到时间词 2. 注意介词的使用，比如at five o'clock（在5点）、on Monday（在周一）、in August（在八月）等
where 地点类	◆ 以Where开头 ◆ 询问考生"去哪儿做什么、去哪儿玩什么"等	1. 听到where开头的问题时，就要回答与地点相关的内容 2. 注意介词的使用，at表示地点时，后面常常接具体的地点，且通常是小的地点，比如at home（在家）
how 方式类	◆ how意为"怎样"，用来询问交通方式、方法等	回答时注意介词的使用，比如by bus（乘公交车）、on foot（步行）
	◆ How do you think of...?询问对方对某事的看法	回答时常用"I think..."
	◆ how之后还可跟形容词 ◆ How long...? 询问多长时间 ◆ How far...? 询问（离……）多远	回答可用It's... 或It takes...
how often 频率类	◆ How often...? 提问频率，意思是"多久一次" ◆ 常问到的问题包括"多久去一次哪里、多久做一次什么"等	答语要包括做某件事情的频率，比如once a week（一周一次）等

常考的问题类型		
问题类型	特点	答题技巧
how many/ how much 数量类	◆ 对数量进行提问 ◆ how many提问时，后面跟可数名词的复数，通常问"多少人、多少天"等 ◆ how much后面跟不可数名词，通常问"多少作业、多少钱"等	回答用There be句型
which 事实选择类	◆ which意为"哪一个""哪一些"，指在一定范围内的某一个，比如which language（哪种语言）、which subject（哪一门课）、which song（哪首歌）等	用完整的句子回答
please tell me 描述类	◆ Please tell me something about...（请告诉我一些关于……）	用2～5句话介绍
	◆ 描述人物	可以从外貌、职业、爱好、相处如何等角度阐述
	◆ 描述喜欢的事物	可以从具体事物、为什么喜欢等角度阐述
	◆ 描述一段经历	可以从发生的时间、地点、做了什么事、心情如何等角度阐述
or 二选一类	◆ 常见句式有两种，A和B二选一 Which is more... A or B? Do you prefer A or B?	1. 回答时不仅要表明选择A还是B，还要说明选择A或B的原因 2. 用2～5句话介绍

Day 5　口语必备技能

一、常用连接词

口语考试中，考生把简单句说好，再搭配一些英语连接词，把它们用自然，用熟练，得高分则不是问题。

常用关键词		举例
表因果	because 因为	My hobby is reading **because** reading is fun. 我的爱好是阅读，因为阅读很有趣。
	so 所以	
	so that 以便，为了	

续表

	常用关键词	举例
表让步	although 虽然，尽管 even if 即使 even though 即使	I am fascinated with dancing, **even if** I have two left feet. 即使我笨手笨脚的，但我很喜欢跳舞。
表转折	but 但是 however 然而 yet 然而	My room was small **but** clean. 我的房间虽小，但很干净。
表递进	especially 尤其，特别 besides 而且	**Besides**, I think this is a relaxing place to hang around. 此外，我觉得这是一个放松的地方。
表对比	while 然而 whereas 然而	I enjoy watching movies, **while** my sister prefers reading books. 我喜欢看电影，而我妹妹喜欢看书。
表举例	like 例如 such as 比如 for example 例如 for instance 例如	I think famous tourist attractions, **like** the Great Wall and the Palace Museum, are worth visiting. 我认为著名的旅游景点，如长城和故宫，值得一游。
表修饰	that作关系代词，引导从句	The most important thing is **that** we always try our best and never give up. 最重要的是，我们总是尽我们最大的努力，永不放弃。
	who表示所指的人	She is a person **who** gives me the impression of being kind and caring. 她给我的印象是善良和体贴。
	why 为什么，……的原因	The reason **why** I admire her is that she is kind and always willing to help others. 我钦佩她的原因是她善良，并且总是愿意帮助别人。
	when当……时候	I first got to know him **when** I was in first grade. 我第一次认识他是在我上一年级的时候。
	if如果	**If** it is bad weather, I might stay at home and do some washing and cleaning. 如果天气不好，我可能会待在家里洗衣服和打扫卫生。

二、常用的5种时态

A2 Key口语常用的5种时态是一般现在时、一般过去时、一般将来时、现在进行时、现在完成时。

常用时态	举例	用法
一般现在时	◆ I **read** books **every day**. 我每天都读书。 ◆ I **think** reading helps people think. 我认为阅读能帮助人们思考。	◆ 描述习惯、兴趣和日常行为 ◆ 描述客观事实 ◆ 表达观点

常用时态	举例	用法
一般过去时	◆ This year, all my families **came** back home. 今年，我所有的家人都回家了。	◆ 描述过去发生的事
一般将来时	◆ I **am going to** the museum with my friends. 我要和朋友们一起去博物馆。	◆ 讲述未来的计划
现在进行时	◆ Online shopping **is becoming** more and more popular. 网购越来越流行了。	◆ 描述正在发生的事
现在完成时	◆ I **have studied** piano for three years. 我学习钢琴3年了。 ◆ I **have been** a football fan for more than 2 years. 我当球迷已经2年多了。	◆ 描述过去的事对现在有影响

三、口语必会句型

A2 Key口语考试中，主要涉及的问题包括两类："喜好类"和"观点类"。考生需要掌握如何询问喜好和意见，以及如何回答喜好类、观点类问题。

1. 问喜好

1) Do you like/enjoy...? 你喜欢······吗？

2) Do you prefer...? 你喜欢······吗？

3) Would you like to...? 你想要······吗？

2. 表达喜欢及原因

1) I like... because/as... 我喜欢······因为······

2) I am keen on... 我喜欢······

3) I'm interested in... 我对······感兴趣。

4) I am a big fan of... 我很喜欢······

5) I am really into ... 我真的很喜欢······

6) I prefer... because/as... 我更喜欢······因为······

7) I'd prefer A to B. 比起B，我更喜欢A。

8) I prefer doing/ to do... 我更喜欢做······

9) I would like to... 我想要······

3. 表达不喜欢及原因

1) I don't like it at all. The reason is that... 我一点也不喜欢它。原因是······

2) I'm afraid I don't like... 恐怕我不喜欢······

3) I'm not into... 我不喜欢······

4. 问意见

1) Do you agree with me? 你同意我的看法吗?

2) Do you think so? 你认为是这样吗?

3) What do you think? 你认为呢?

4) Do you think that's a good idea? 你认为这是个好主意吗?

5) What about you? 你觉得呢?

6) What's your opinion? 你的意见呢?

7) Shall we...? 我们······好吗?

5. 表达观点

1) I think... 我认为······

2) In my opinion, ... 在我看来，······

3) It seems to me that... 在我看来······

4) I'm not so sure about that, but... 我不太确定，但是······

5) We'd better... 我们最好······

6. 表示赞同

1) I agree. 我同意。

2) Yes, I agree with you. 是的，我同意你的看法。

3) Well, yes, I suppose you're right. 是的，我想你说得对。

4) Yes, I think so, too. 是的，我也这么认为。

5) I suppose so. 我想是这样。

6) I really like that idea! 我真的很喜欢这个主意!

7) That sounds great! 听起来很棒!

8) That's a good/smart idea. 那是个好主意。

9) That's great. 太好了。

10) That's interesting. 那很有趣。

11) That's wonderful. 棒极了。

7. 表示不赞同

1) I don't agree with you because... 我不同意你的看法，因为······

2) Maybe yes, but I... 也许如此，但我······

3) I don't think so. 我不这么认为。

4) I don't think that's a good idea because... 我认为那不是个好主意，因为……

5) I don't think so because... 我不这么认为，因为……

6) That's good/not bad, but... 那很好/不错，但是……

8. 救场用语

1) Could you say that again, please? 请您再说一遍好吗？

2) Could you please say it again? 您能再说一遍吗？

3) Could you repeat that please? 请您重复一遍好吗？

Weekend 二 每周一练

为帮助考生快速熟悉考试题型和内容，我们提供了中英文对照的官方样题。通过这种方式，我们希望能够帮助考生更好地理解题目，并提高应试能力。

Part 1 官方样题

Part 1 (3~4 minutes)

Phase 1 阶段 1

Interlocutor 考官

To both candidates（对两名考生说）	Good morning / afternoon / evening. 早上好/下午好/晚上好。
	Can I have your mark sheets, please? 请把你的评分表给我好吗？
	Hand over the mark sheets to the Assessor. 把评分表递给评分老师。
	I'm..., and this is... 我是……，这位是……
To Candidate A 对考生A说	What's your name? 你叫什么名字？
To Candidate B 对考生B说	And what's your name? 你叫什么名字？
	Back-up prompts 备选提示
	B, how old are you? 考生B，你多大了？

For UK, ask	Where do you come from?	Are you from (Spain, etc.)?
对英国人，询问：	你来自哪里？	你来自（西班牙……）吗？
For Non UK, ask	Where do you live?	Do you live in…(name of district / town etc.)
对非英国人，询问：	你住在哪里？	你住在……（地区/城镇名字）吗？

Thank you. 谢谢。

A, how old are you?

考生A，你多大了？

For UK, ask	Where do you come from?	Are you from (Spain, etc.)?
对英国人，询问：	你来自哪里？	你来自（西班牙……）吗？
For Non-UK, ask	Where do you live?	Do you live in (name of district / town etc.)?
对非英国人，询问：	你住在哪里？	你住在……（地区/城镇名字）吗？

Thank you. 谢谢。

Phase 2 阶段 2

Interlocutor 考官

Now, let's talk about school. 现在，让我们谈谈学校。

Back-up prompts 备选提示

A, what subject do you like best?

考生A，你最喜欢什么学科？

Do you like maths?

你喜欢数学吗？

What clothes do you wear to school?

你上学穿什么衣服？

Do you wear a uniform?

你穿校服吗？

B, What time do you finish school?

考生B，你什么时候放学？

Do you finish school at 4 o'clock?

你是四点放学吗？

What do you eat after school?

放学后你吃什么？

Do you eat snacks after school?

你放学后吃零食吗？

Extended Response 拓展回答

Now A, please tell me something about the homework you have to do.

现在，考生A，请告诉我你不得不做的家庭作业。

Back-up questions 备选问题

Do you get a lot of homework every day?

你每天有很多家庭作业吗？

Did you do any homework yesterday?

你昨天做作业了吗？

Do you like homework? (Why?/Why not?)

你喜欢家庭作业吗？（为什么？/为什么不？）

Interlocutor 考官

Now, let's talk about home. 现在，让我们谈谈家。

B, Who do you live with?

考生B，你和谁住在一起？

How many bedrooms are there in your house?

你家有几间卧室？

A, Where do you watch TV at home?

考生A，在家时，你在哪儿看电视？

What's your favourite room in your house?

你最喜欢家里的哪个房间？

Extended Response 拓展回答

Now, B, please tell me what you like doing at home.

现在，考生B，请告诉我你在家里喜欢做什么。

Back-up prompts 备选提示

Do you live with your family?

你和你的家人住在一起吗？

Are there three bedrooms in your house?

你家有三间卧室吗？

Do you watch TV in the kitchen?

你在厨房看电视吗？

Do you like your bedroom?

你喜欢你的卧室吗？

Back-up questions 备选问题

Do you like cooking?

你喜欢做饭吗？

Do you play computer games?

你玩电脑游戏吗？

Did you stay at home last weekend?

上周末你在家待着吗？

Part 2 官方样题

Part 2 (5～6 minutes)

Do you like these different hobbies? Say why or why not.

你喜欢这些不同的爱好吗？说说为什么或为什么不。

Phase 1 阶段 1

Interlocutor 考官

3-4 minutes 3 ~ 4 分钟

Now, in this part of the test you are going to talk together.

现在，在这一部分考试中，你们将一起讨论。

(*Place Part 2 booklet, open at Task 2, in front of candidates.*)

（将第2部分的小册子，在任务2处打开，放在考生面前。）

Here are some pictures that show different hobbies.

这里有一些展示不同爱好的图片。

Do you like these different hobbies? Say why or why not.

你喜欢这些不同的爱好吗？说出为什么或为什么不。

I'll say that again. 我再说一遍。

Do you like these different hobbies? Say why or why not.

你喜欢这些不同的爱好吗？说出为什么或为什么不。

All right? Now, talk together. 好了吗？现在，一起讨论吧。

Candidates 考生 ···

🕐 *Allow a minimum of 1 minute (maximum of 2 minutes)*
before moving on to the following questions

答题时间最少1分钟（最多2分钟），然后再进入下面的问题。

Interlocutor 考官/

Candidates 考生

Use as appropriate.

Ask each candidate

at least one

question.

（酌情使用，询问每个考生至少一个问题）

Do you think... 你认为……

... playing football is fun? ……踢足球有趣吗？

... playing an instrument is difficult? 演奏乐器困难吗？

... playing computer games is boring? 玩电脑游戏无聊吗？

... reading is interesting? 阅读有趣吗？

... painting/drawing is easy? 画画容易吗？

> **Optional prompt 可选提示**
>
> Why? / Why not?
>
> 为什么？/为什么不?
>
> What do you think?
>
> 你怎么认为？

Interlocutor 考官

So, A, which of these hobbies do you like best?

所以，考生A，这些爱好中，你最喜欢哪一个？

And you, B, which of these hobbies do you like best?

你呢，考生B，这些爱好中，你最喜欢哪一个？

Thank you. (Can I have the booklet, please?)

谢谢。（请把小册子给我好吗？）

（*Retrieve Part 2 booklet. 收回第2部分的小册子。*）

Phase 2 阶段 2

Interlocutor 考官

Now, do you prefer to spend your free time alone or with other people, B? (Why?)

现在，你更喜欢在空闲时间独处还是和其他人在一起，考生B？（为什么？）

🕐 *Allow up to 2 minutes*

答题时间最多2分钟

And what about you, A? (Do you prefer to spend your free time alone or with other people?) (Why?)

你呢，考生A？（你更喜欢在空闲时间独处还是和其他人在一起？）（为什么？）

Which is more fun, playing sports or watching sports, A? (Why?)

参加体育运动和观看体育比赛哪个更有趣，考生A？（为什么？）

And you, B? (Which is more fun, playing sports or watching sports?) (Why?)

你呢，考生B？（参加体育运动和观看体育比赛哪个更有趣？）（为什么？）

Thank you. That is the end of the test.

谢谢。考试到此结束。

Week 2

Part 1 个人信息

考试模块	时间	话题	我是考官	我是考生	
			第2周目标		
Part 1 Phase 1 个人信息	Day 1	问候	How are you doing?	I'm doing fine.	☐
	Day 2	姓名	What's your name?	My name is... I am...	☐
	Day 3	年龄	How old are you?	I am ... (years old).	☐
	Day 4	来自哪里	Where are you from?	I am from...	☐
	Day 5	家和家人	Do you live with your family?	Yes, I live with...	☐
	Weekend	每周一练	每周基础知识练习		☐

Day 1 问候

 考场模拟

 Good morning. Can I have your mark sheets, please? I'm Mary, and this is Claire.

How are you doing?

I'm doing fine.

 思路点拨

Q: **How are you doing?** 你好吗?

I'm doing fine. 我很好。

*回答可以用I'm doing fine.或者I'm fine.都可以。不建议用消极、非积极的回答，比如，Not so good.（不是特别好）、Not so bad.（不算很坏）、Not bad.（不坏）、Just so so.（就那样）。这样的回答可能会引发考官继续询问：Why so?（为什么感觉不好呢？）

 考点锦囊

"问候"常见问答	
Q我是考官	A我是考生
Good morning. 早上好。	Good morning. 早上好。
Good afternoon.下午好。	Good afternoon.下午好。
Hello! 你好!	Hello! 你好!
Hi! 你好!	Hi! 你好!
How do you do? 你好!	How do you do? 你好!
Nice to meet you. 很高兴认识你。	Nice to meet you, too. 我也很高兴认识你。
Glad to see you. 很高兴认识你。	Glad to see you, too. 我也很高兴认识你。
How are you? 你好吗?	I'm fine. Thanks. 我很好，谢谢。
	Fine. 很好。
	I'm pretty good. 我非常好。
	Pretty good. 非常好。
How's it going? 最近怎么样?	I'm great! 我好极了!
	I'm very good! 我好极了!
How's everything? 一切还好吧?	Couldn't be better. 好得不能再好了。
What's up? 你好吗?	Nothing special. 没什么特别。
	All good. 一切都好。
Are you well? 你好吗?	I'm pretty well. 我非常好。

★必会句型★

1. 问候——询问对方

1) How do you do? 你好!

2) How are you? 你好吗?

3) How's it going? 最近怎么样?

4) How's everything? 一切还好吧?

5) Good morning, sir/madam. 早上好,先生/女士。

6) IIow arc you doing? 你好吗?

7) Nice to meet you. 很高兴认识你。

8) Glad to see you. 很高兴认识你。

2. 问候——回应对方

1) I'm fine. 我很好。

2) I'm pretty good. 我非常好。

3) I'm great! 我好极了!

4) I'm very good! 我好极了!

5) I'm fine. Thanks. 我很好,谢谢。

6) All good. 一切都好。

7) Couldn't be better. 好得不能再好了。

8) Nice to meet you, too. 我也很高兴认识你。

Day 2 姓名

 考场模拟

 Good morning. Can I have your mark sheets, please? I'm Mary, and this is Claire.

What's your name, please?

My name is Wang Ming.

思路点拨

Q: What's your name, please? 请问你叫什么名字?

My name is / I am _____. 我的名字是_____。

*考生要用真实姓名作答，考官会据此核实考生姓名。中文名字的英文写法姓在前、名在前两种形式都可以。

 ## 考点锦囊

"姓名" 常见问答	
Q我是考官	A我是考生
May I know your name, please? 我可以知道你的名字吗？	Sure, my name is Li Ming. 当然，我的名字是李明。
Do you have an English name? 你有英文名字吗？	Yes, it's Peter. 有的，彼得。
What's your English name? 你的英文名是什么？	My English name is Helen. 我的英文名是海伦。
What's your surname/ family name? 你姓什么？	It's Wu. 我姓吴。
What's your full name? 你的全名叫什么？	My full name is Han Mei. 我的全名是韩梅。
Can you spell your name, please? 你能拼写一下你的名字吗？	Yes, it's W-A-N-G M-I-N-G. 好的，W-A-N-G M-I-N-G。
How do you spell your surname? 你的姓怎么拼写？	J-I-N. J-I-N。

"姓名" 高阶问答	
Q我是考官	A我是考生
What is the meaning of your name? 你的名字有什么含义？	The meaning of my name is "helpful". 我名字的意思是"乐于助人"。
	My name represents a kind and caring nature. 我的名字代表了一种善良和关怀的天性。
Does your name have any special meaning? 你的名字有什么特别的含义吗？	Yes. My parents want me to be brave. 是的，我的父母希望我勇敢。
	Yes. It is from a great ancient poetry in China. 是的，它取自一首伟大的中国古诗。

名字含义		
kindness 善良	helpful 乐于助人的	brave 勇敢的
courage 勇敢	beautiful 漂亮的	careful 仔细的
wisdom 智慧	polite 有礼貌的	proud 自豪的
honesty 诚实	excellent 优秀的	rich 富有的

★**必会句型**★

1. 介绍名字

1) I'm... 我是……

2) My name is... 我的名字是……

3) My English name is... 我的英文名字是……

4) My surname is... 我姓……

5) My family name is... 我姓……

6) My full name is... 我的全名是……

2. 名字拼写

1) It's W-A-N-G H-A-O. W-A-N-G H-A-O。（*回答名字拼写时，要读英文字母而不是拼音）

2) W-A-N-G. W-A-N-G。

3. 名字含义

1) The meaning of my name is... 我名字的意思是……

2) My name represents a ... nature. 我的名字代表了一种……的天性。

3) My parents want me to be... 我的父母希望我成为……

4) It is from a great ancient poetry in China. 它取自一首伟大的中国古诗。

Day 3 年龄

 考场模拟

 Good morning. Can I have your mark sheets, please? I'm Mary, and this is Claire.

How old are you?

I'm 11/ eleven years old.

思路点拨

Q: **How old are you? 你多大了？**

I am _____ (years old). 我_____岁。

*建议用完整的句子回答考官的问题，不要只回答数字，其中years old可以省略，比如，"我11岁"，可以直接说成I am eleven。

考点锦囊

"年龄"常见问答	
Q我是考官	**A我是考生**
How old are you? 你多大了？	I'm **ten** years old. 我10岁了。
When were you born? 你什么时候出生的？	I was born in **2012**. 我出生于2012年。
What is your date of birth? 你的出生日期是什么时候？	I was born on **June 1st**. 我出生于6月1日。
When is your birthday? 你的生日是什么时候？	My birthday is on **October 10th**. 我的生日是10月10日。

"年龄"回答公式	
回答年龄	**回答出生年月日**
I'm + 基数词	月份 + 日期序数词 + 年份
	日期序数词 + of + 月份 + 年份
I'm + 基数词 + years old	如2012年10月1日 读成： October the first, two thousand and twelve 或 the first of October, two thousand and twelve
*in用在年份或者月份前面；on用在具体的日期前面	

基数词：描述事物数量多少的数词		
1~10	**11~19**	**20~100**
one 1	eleven 11	
two 2	twelve 12	twen**ty** 20
three 3	thir**teen** 13	thir**ty** 30
four 4	four**teen** 14	for**ty** 40

续表

基数词：描述事物数量多少的数词		
1 ~ 10	11 ~ 19	20 ~ 100
five 5	fif**teen** 15	fif**ty** 50
six 6	six**teen** 16	six**ty** 60
seven 7	seven**teen** 17	seven**ty** 70
eight 8	eigh**teen** 18	eigh**ty** 80
nine 9	nine**teen** 19	nine**ty** 90
ten 10		hundred 100

序数词： 表示顺序的数词		
第1 ~ 10	第11 ~ 19	第20 ~ 100
first 第1	eleven**th** 第11	
second 第2	twelf**th** 第12	twentie**th** 第20
third 第3	thirteen**th** 第13	thirtie**th** 第30
four**th** 第4	fourteen**th** 第14	fortie**th** 第40
fif**th** 第5	fifteen**th** 第15	fiftie**th** 第50
six**th** 第6	sixteen**th** 第16	sixtie**th** 第60
seven**th** 第7	seventeen**th** 第17	seventie**th** 第70
eigh**th** 第8	eighteen**th** 第18	eightie**th** 第80
nin**th** 第9	nineteen**th** 第19	ninetie**th** 第90
ten**th** 第10		hundred**th** 第100

十二个月			
January 一月	April 四月	July 七月	October 十月
February 二月	May 五月	August 八月	November 十一月
March 三月	June 六月	September 九月	December 十二月

★必会句型★

1. **介绍年龄**

1) I am ... years old. 我……岁了。

2) I am ... 我……岁了。

2. 介绍出生年月日

1) I was born in...（年份）我出生于……

2) I was born on...（月份 + 日期）我出生在……

3) My birthday is... 我的生日是……

Day 4 来自哪里

 考场模拟

 Good morning. Can I have your mark sheets, please? I'm Mary, and this is Claire.

Where are you from?

I am from Shanghai.

 思路点拨

Q: **Where are you from? 你来自哪里?**

I am from _____. 我来自_____。

*考生只需要回答省份名或城市名即可，不需要回答详细住址。

 考点锦囊

"来自哪里" 常见问答	
Q我是考官	A我是考生
Where do you come from? 你来自哪里?	I come from Beijing. 我来自北京。
	I'm from Nanjing. 我来自南京。
Are you from Shanghai? 你来自上海吗?	Yes, I am from Shanghai. 是的，我来自上海。
	No, I come from Guangzhou. 不是，我来自广州。

"来自哪里"常见问答	
Q我是考官	A我是考生
Which city do you come from? 你来自哪个城市?	I come from Tianjin. 我来自天津。
Where do you live? 你住在哪里?	I live in Beijing. 我住在北京。
Do you live in Beijing? 你住在北京吗?	Yes, I live in Beijing. 是的,我住在北京。
	No, I live in Hebei. 不,我住在河北。

居住地		
地域	街区	房子
capital city 首都	city centre 市中心	house 房子
province 省份	downtown 市区	home 家;住所
city 城市	district 区域	housing estate 住宅区
town 城镇	block 街区	flat 公寓
suburb 郊区,城郊	neighbourhood 街区,四邻	apartment 公寓
countryside 乡村		cottage 别墅
village 村庄		studio 工作室
rural area 农村地区		
farm 农场		

★必会句型★

介绍居住地

1) I am from... 我来自……

2) I come from... 我来自……

3) I live in... 我住在……

Day 5　家和家人

考场模拟

Good morning. Can I have your mark sheets, please? I'm Mary, and this is Claire.

Do you live with your family?

Yes, I live with my parents.

思路点拨

Q:　Do you live with your family? 你和家人住在一起吗?

Yes, I live with ＿＿＿＿＿＿＿＿＿＿＿＿＿.

是的，我跟＿＿＿＿＿＿＿＿＿＿＿＿＿住在一起。

*考生根据实际情况作答即可，比如爸爸妈妈、爷爷奶奶或者外公外婆。

考点锦囊

"家和家人"常见问答	
Q我是考官	A我是考生
Who do you live with? 你和谁住在一起?	I live with **my parents**. 我和父母住在一起。
Where do the people in your family live? 你的家人住在哪里?	My family lives in **an apartment**. 我们全家住在一个公寓里。
How many people are there in your family? 你家有几口人?	There are **four** people in my family. They are my father, mother, sister and I. 我们家有四口人，他们是我的爸爸、妈妈、姐姐和我。
How many brothers and sisters do you have? 你有几个兄弟姐妹?	I have **no brothers or sisters**. 我没有兄弟姐妹。
	I'm **the only child** in my family. 我是家里的独生子。
	I just have **one sister**. 我只有一个姐姐（妹妹）。
	I just have **one brother**. 我只有一个哥哥（弟弟）。

续表

"家和家人"常见问答	
Q我是考官	A我是考生
Who is the oldest person in your family? 你家里谁年纪最大?	My **dad** is the oldest. 我爸爸是年纪最大的。
When is your father's birthday? 你爸爸的生日是什么时候?	My father's birthday is **on March 2nd**. 我爸爸的生日在3月2日。
When is your mother's birthday? 你妈妈的生日是什么时候?	My mother's birthday is **on September 9th**. 我妈妈的生日在9月9日。

家庭成员			
dad 爸爸	grand(d)ad 爷爷;外公	uncle 叔叔;伯父	grandson 外孙;孙子
mum 妈妈	grandfather 爷爷;外公	aunt 姑母;姨母	granddaughter(外)孙女
parents 父母	grandma 奶奶;外婆	cousin 堂兄弟姐妹	son 儿子
brother 哥哥,弟弟	grandmother 奶奶;外婆	nephew 侄子;外甥	daughter 女儿
sister 姐姐,妹妹	grandparent 祖父(母);外祖父(母)	niece 外甥女;侄女	

家庭成员数量		
only child 独生子(女)	an elder sister 一个姐姐	one child 一个孩子
no brothers or sisters 没有兄弟姐妹	a younger sister 一个妹妹	two children 两个孩子
	an elder brother 一个哥哥	three children 三个孩子
	a younger brother 一个弟弟	

★必会句型★

1. 介绍"和谁住在一起"

I live with... 我和……住在一起。

2. 介绍"家人住在哪里"

They live in... 他们住在……

3. 介绍"家里成员"

1) There are... in my family. 我家里有……

2) I have no brothers or sisters. 我没有兄弟姐妹。

3) I'm the only child in my family. 我是家里的独生子。

4) I just have one ... 我只有一个……

Weekend 二 每周一练

I. 选一选，选出最合适的答语。

( ) 1. Q: How many people are there in your family?

A) There are three people.

B) I am from Beijing.

C) I am eleven years old.

( ) 2. Q: Where do you come from?

A) How do you do?

B) My English name is Lucy.

C) I come from Guangzhou.

( ) 3. Q: How is it going?

A) I live with my parents.

B) I am fine. Thank you.

C) I am ten years old.

( ) 4. Q: How old are you?

A) I'm very good!

B) Yes, it's Jimmy.

C) I'm twelve years old.

( ) 5. Q: What is your date of birth?

A) Nice to meet you, too.

B) I was born on Sep. 10th, 2012.

C) I am from Shanghai.

( ) 6. Q: Where do you live?

A) I'm great.

B) I live in Chongqing.

C) My English name is Sally.

II. 读一读，圈出正确的单词。

1. My name *are / is* Hu Liang.

2. My friends live *near / nears* me.

3. I'm thirteen *years / year* old.

4. Glad to *see / sees* you.

5. Do you have *an / a* English name?

6. When *were / are* you born?

7. Which city *do / does* you come from?

8. Does your name have *some / any* special meaning?

9. How are you *do / doing*?

10. How do you spell *your / you* surname?

III. 将左右两列的相应内容连线，构成完整的一句话。

1. My	A. no brothers or sisters.
2. I have	B. given name's Mingming.
3. I'm eleven	C. from China.
4. I come	D. years old.
5. I'm	E. on Jan. 6th, 2013.
6. I was born	F. doing fine.
7. I live	G. is the oldest.
8. My dad	H. in Shanghai.

IV. 判断下面句子正误，如有错，请圈出并将正确形式写在下面的横线上。

1. I just have one sisters. ☐

_____

2. Where are you come from? ☐

_____

3. When were you born? ☐

_____

4. What do you spell your first name? ☐

_____

5. How old is you? ☐

_____

6. What are your full name? ☐

_____

7. Were you born on this city? ☐

_____

8. How many people is there in your family? ☐

_____

V. 连词成句。

1. name / is / your/ What /?

_____

2. is / given / My / name / Yang /.

_____

3. you / China / from / Are /?

_____

4. city / in / live / this / They /.

_____

5. were / you / When / born /?

_____

6. your / Where / is / birthplace /?

_____

7. pretty / I / good / am /.

_____

8. spell / do / How / you / it /?

_____

VI. 模拟演练。

>>Activity 1

Examiner: Good morning. Can I have your mark sheets, please? I'm Jenny and this is Kate. How are you doing?

Candidate A/B: 1. _____

Examiner: What's your name, please?

Candidate A/B: 2. _____

Examiner: When were you born?

Candidate A/B: 3. _____

Examiner: Where do you come from?

Candidate A/B: 4. _____

>>Activity 2

Examiner: Good morning. Can I have your mark sheets, please? I'm Jake and this is Leo. May I have your name, please?

Candidate A/B: 5. _____

Examiner: How old are you?

Candidate A/B: 6. _____

Examiner: Are you from Beijing?

Candidate A/B: 7. _____

Examiner: Do you live with your family?

Candidate A/B: 8. _____

Part 1 日常生活

	第3周目标				
考试模块	时间	话题	我是考官	我是考生	
Part 1 Phase 2 日常生活	Day 1	食物	What's your favourite food?	I like... very much because...	☐
	Day 2	语言	When did you start learning English?	I started learning English when I was... (years old).	☐
	Day 3	天气	What's the weather like today?	It is...	☐
	Day 4	学校	Which school are you studying at?	I am studying at...	☐
	Day 5	服装	What clothes do you wear to school?	I usually wear... to school.	☐
	Weekend	每周一练	每周基础知识练习		☐

Day 1　食物

 考场模拟

 Now, let's talk about **food**.

What's your favourite food?

I like Chinese food very much because I like dumplings.

思路点拨

Q: **What's your favourite food? 你最喜欢的食物是什么？**

I like _____ very much because _____ .

我很喜欢 _____ 因为 _____ 。

*当考官问"喜欢"类问题时，考生可以补充回答"为什么"，即从原因的角度进行扩展。

考点锦囊

"食物"常见问答	
Q我是考官	A我是考生
Do you eat vegetables every week? 你每周都吃蔬菜吗？	Yes, I eat vegetables every week. 是的，我每周都吃蔬菜。
Where does your family buy food? 你们家在哪里买食物？	My family always buys food in the supermarket. 我的家人总是在超市买食物。
What kind of food do you like best? Why? 你最喜欢吃什么？为什么？	I like pizza best because it is delicious and cheesy. 我最喜欢比萨，因为它既美味又有奶酪味。
What is your favourite fruit? Why? 你最喜欢的水果是什么？为什么？	My favourite fruit is apple. I like it because it is crunchy and juicy. 我最喜欢的水果是苹果。我喜欢它，因为它又脆又多汁。
Which of these drinks: coca cola, sprite, orange juice etc. do you like best? 你最喜欢以下哪一种饮料：可口可乐、雪碧、橙汁？	I like orange juice best because it tastes good. 我最喜欢橙汁，因为橙汁味道很好。

"一日三餐"常见问答	
Q我是考官	A我是考生
What time do you have dinner every day? 你每天几点吃晚饭？	I have dinner at six o'clock in the evening every day. 我每天晚上六点吃晚饭。
What do you usually have for breakfast? 你早餐通常吃什么？	I usually have bread and milk for breakfast. 我早餐通常吃面包和牛奶。

"食物"高阶问答	
Q我是考官	A我是考生
Do you think drinking hot chocolate is healthy? 你认为喝热巧克力健康吗？	Yes, I do. Drinking hot chocolate can give people energy. 是的，喝热巧克力可以给人能量。

"食物"高阶问答	
Q我是考官	A我是考生
Do you think making cakes is difficult? 你认为做蛋糕难吗?	Yes, it always takes me too much time to make cakes. And the process of making cakes is also complicated. 是的，做蛋糕总是花费我太多的时间。制作蛋糕的过程也很复杂。
Do you prefer to make cakes with your friends or with your mum? 你更喜欢和朋友还是和妈妈一起做蛋糕?	I prefer to make cakes with my mum because she is good at making cakes and I can learn from her. 我更喜欢和妈妈一起做蛋糕，因为她擅长做蛋糕，我可以向她学习。
Please tell me something about a meal that you enjoy eating. 请告诉我你喜欢吃的一顿饭。	I like breakfast because it's the first meal of a day. For breakfast, I usually have an egg, some bread, and a glass of milk. 我喜欢早餐，因为它是一天中的第一餐。早餐我通常吃一个鸡蛋、一些面包和一杯牛奶。

各种食物			
主食	肉蛋	蔬菜	水果
cereal 谷类食物	chicken 鸡肉	bean 豆	apple 苹果
bread 面包	fish 鱼肉	carrot 胡萝卜	banana 香蕉
flour 面粉	meat 肉	cabbage 卷心菜	pear 梨
noodle 面条	beef 牛肉	broccoli 西蓝花	orange 橙子
rice 大米	lamb 羊肉	potato 土豆	lemon 柠檬
burger 汉堡包	egg 鸡蛋	mushroom 蘑菇	grape 葡萄

零食	饮料	三餐
biscuit 饼干	water 水	meal 一餐
cake 蛋糕	tea 茶	breakfast 早餐
can 罐头	coffee 咖啡	lunch 午餐
candy 糖果	juice 果汁	dinner 晚餐
cheese 奶酪	orange juice 橙汁	supper 晚餐
chocolate 巧克力	soda 苏打水	have breakfast 吃早餐
potato chip 薯片	milk 牛奶	have lunch 吃午餐
cookie 曲奇饼	hot chocolate 热巧克力	have dinner 吃晚餐
chips 炸薯条	lemonade 柠檬水	delicious food 美味的食物
popcorn 爆米花	cola 可乐	
ice cream 冰激凌	yogurt 酸奶	

续表

零食	饮料	三餐
donuts 甜甜圈		
nuts 坚果		

★必会句型★

1. 介绍喜欢的食物

1) I like... 我喜欢……

2) I love... 我喜欢……

3) I like... best, because... 我最喜欢……，因为……

4) I like... very much because... 我很喜欢……因为……

5) My favourite food is... 我最喜欢的食物是……

6) My favourite fruit is... 我最喜欢的水果是……

7) My favourite drink is... 我最喜欢的饮料是……

2. 介绍一日三餐

1) For breakfast, I usually have... 早餐我通常吃……

2) I usually have ... for lunch. 我午餐通常吃……

3) I usually have ... for dinner. 我晚餐通常吃……

4) I have dinner at ... o'clock in the evening every day. 我每天晚上……点吃晚饭。

5) I like breakfast because it's the first meal of a day. 我喜欢早餐，因为它是一天的第一餐。

Day 2　语言

 考场模拟

Now, let's talk about **language**.

When did you start learning English?

I started learning English when I was five years old.

思路点拨

Q: **When did you start learning English? 你什么时候开始学习英语的?**

I started learning English when I was _____ (years old).

我_____岁时开始学习英语。

*当问到过去的时间时，动词要用过去式。

 考点锦囊

"语言" 常见问答	
Q我是考官	A我是考生
How long have you studied English? 你学习英语多久了?	I have studied English for about six years. 我学英语大约有六年了。
When did you start learning English? 你什么时候开始学习英语的?	I started learning English when I was five years old. 我5岁时开始学英语。
Which foreign language are you studying at your school? 你在学校学习哪门外语?	I am studying English at my school. 我在学校学习英语。
Do you read English every day? 你每天都读英语吗?	Yes, I read English every day. 是的，我每天都读英语。
Is English hard or easy for you? 英语对你来说困难还是容易?	It is a bit difficult for me. 英语对我来说有点儿难。
Which language is spoken in your country? 你们国家的人讲哪种语言?	In China, people speak Chinese. 在中国，人们讲汉语。
How many languages can you understand? 你能听懂几种语言?	Two. I can understand both Chinese and English. 两种。我能听懂汉语和英语。

"语言" 高阶问答	
Q我是考官	A我是考生
What do you find difficult about learning English? 你觉得在学习英语方面有什么困难吗?	I find English grammar difficult. I always make mistakes. 我觉得英语语法很难。我经常出错。
Do you like learning English? Why? 你喜欢学习英语吗? 为什么?	Yes, I do because I love travelling to foreign countries and communicating with others in English. 是的，我喜欢学习英语。因为我喜欢去国外旅游，喜欢用英语和别人交流。

学习某种语言的原因	
interested in the language 对语言感兴趣	prepare oneself for an international education 为国外求学做好准备

续表

学习某种语言的原因	
love travelling to foreign countries 喜欢去国外旅游	for a better school 为了更好的学校
gain a better sense of the world 更好地了解世界	expand one's knowledge 扩展知识
communicate with others 与他人交流	acquire bilingual ability 获得双语能力
understand other cultures 了解其他文化	explore a different culture 探索不同的文化

★必会句型★

1. 介绍学习语言的时间

1) I have studied English for... years. 我学英语……年了。

2) I started learning English when I was ... years old. 我……岁时开始学英语。

2. 介绍学习语言的类别

I am studying ... at my school. 我在学校学习……

3. 介绍学习语言的难易

1) It is a bit difficult for me. 这对我来说有点儿难。

2) I find English grammar difficult. 我觉得英语语法很难。

3) I can understand both Chinese and English. 我能听懂汉语和英语。

4. 介绍喜欢某种语言的原因

I do love learning... because I love travelling to foreign countries and communicating with others in ... 我很喜欢学习……，因为我喜欢去国外旅游，喜欢用……和别人交流。

Day 3   天气

考场模拟

Now, let's talk about **weather**.
What's the weather like today?

It's sunny.

思路点拨

Q: What's the weather like today? 今天天气怎么样?

It is _____.

今天是_____。

*根据实际情况作答即可，比如"今天是晴天。"可以回答It is sunny（英语中it用来指代天气）。

 考点锦囊

"天气"常见问答	
Q我是考官	**A我是考生**
How is the weather outside? 外面的天气怎么样?	It is raining outside. 外面正在下雨。
Is it sunny today? 今天晴朗吗? Is it cloudy today? 今天多云吗? Is it windy today? 今天有风吗? Is it snowing today? 今天在下雪吗? Is it raining today? 今天在下雨吗?	Yes, it is. 是的。
	No, it isn't. 不是。
Do you know what the forecast is for tomorrow? 你知道明天的天气预报吗?	Yes, I know. The weather forecast says it will be sunny tomorrow. 是的，我知道。天气预报说明天是晴天。
Will it be warm tomorrow? 明天会暖和吗?	Maybe it will be warm tomorrow. 也许明天会暖和。
	I'm not sure, but I hope it will be warm tomorrow. 我不确定，但我希望明天会暖和。

"天气"高阶问答	
Q我是考官	**A我是考生**
Can you describe the weather today? 你能描述一下今天的天气吗?	It's windy today. A little bit cold. 今天刮风。有点儿冷。
Do you think that the weather affects people? 你认为天气对人会有影响吗?	Yes, I think so. As we all know, there are not so many outdoor activities in rainy days. While on sunny days people can go outside and have fun. 是的，我想是的。我们都知道，雨天没有那么多的户外活动。而在阳光明媚的日子里，人们可以在户外玩得很开心。

"季节"高阶问答	
Q我是考官	A我是考生
What season do you like best? What do you do in that season? 你最喜欢什么季节？你在那个季节里做什么？	My favourite season is winter. I can go skating with my friends. 我最喜欢的季节是冬天。我可以和朋友去滑冰。
What season do you think is the most suitable for work and study? 你认为什么季节最适合工作和学习？	I think it is autumn. It's not so hot or so cold, and autumn is a season with beautiful scenery. 我想是秋天。秋天不热也不冷，还是一个风景优美的季节。
Which place do you prefer, a place with the same climate all year, or a place that has different seasonal climates? 气候全年一样的地方和气候四季不同的地方，你更喜欢哪里？	I prefer a place with different seasonal climates because only in this way can the landscape in the city be various. If it's the same all year round, it would be very boring. 我更喜欢气候四季不同的地方，因为只有这样，城市景观才能多样化。如果一年到头都是一样的，那就太无聊了。

天气现象		
wind 风	rain 雨	sun 太阳
breeze 微风	snow 雪	sunshine 阳光
hurricane 飓风	sleet 雨夹雪	rainbow 彩虹
tornado 龙卷风	storm 暴风雨	cloud 云
fog 雾	hail 冰雹	thunder 雷
mist 薄雾	lightning 闪电	thunderstorm 雷暴

描述天气的形容词			
春	夏	秋	冬
sunny 阳光充足的	hot 热的	windy 多风的	snowy 被雪覆盖的
clear 晴朗的	rainy 多雨的	foggy 多雾的	icy 冰冷的
warm 温暖的	wet 潮湿的	cloudy 多云的	dry 干燥的
mild 温和的		cool 凉爽的	

★必会句型★

1. 介绍天气情况

1) It is ... outside. 外面正在……

2) It is ... today. 今天（天气）……

3) A little bit ... 有点……

2. 介绍最喜欢的季节

1) My favourite season is ... 我最喜欢的季节是……

2) I can ... with my friends. 我可以和朋友一起……

3) ... is a season with beautiful scenery. ……是一个风景优美的季节。

4) I prefer a place with different ... 我喜欢有着不同……的地方。

5) If it's the same all year round, it would be ... 如果一年到头都是一样的，那就……了。

 Day 4 学校

 考场模拟

Now, let's talk about **school**.

Which school are you studying at?

I am studying at Cuiwei Primary School.

 思路点拨

Q: **Which school are you studying at? 你在哪个学校上学？**

I am studying at _____.

我在_____上学。

*建议考生在考前熟记自己学校的英文名称。

考点锦囊

"学校"常见问答	
Q我是考官	A我是考生
Which grade are you in? 你在几年级？	I am in Grade Five. 我在五年级。

续表

"学校"常见问答	
Q我是考官	A我是考生
Which class are you in? 你在哪个班？	I am in Class One. 我在一班。
How many students are there in your class? 你们班有多少名学生？	There are forty students in our class. 我们班有40名学生。
Can you finish your homework by yourself? 你能自己完成作业吗？	Yes, I often finish my homework by myself. 是的，我经常独立完成作业。
Which middle school do you want to attend? Why? 你想上哪所中学？为什么？	I would like to attend XXX Middle School because it has a strong academic program and excellent after-school activities. 我想上XXX中学，因为它有很强的学术课程和优秀的课外活动。

"上学时间"常见问答	
Q我是考官	A我是考生
When do you go to school every day? 你每天几点去上学？	I go to school at 8 o'clock every day. 我每天八点去上学。
When do you come home from school every day? 你每天什么时候放学回家？	I come home from school at five o'clock in the afternoon every day. 我每天下午五点放学回家。
When does your first lesson start? 你的第一节课几点开始？	My first lesson starts at half past eight. 我的第一节课八点半开始。
How many hours of sports do you have in school? 你在学校有多少小时的体育活动时间？	I have two hours of sports in school. 我在学校有两个小时的体育活动时间。

"科目"常见问答	
Q我是考官	A我是考生
Do you like maths? 你喜欢数学吗？	Yes, I do. Maths is interesting. 是的，我喜欢。数学很有趣。
How often do you have Chinese lessons? 你多久上一次语文课？	I have Chinese lessons four times a week. 我一周上四次语文课。
What is your favourite subject? Why? 你最喜欢的科目是什么？为什么？	My favourite subject is maths because I enjoy solving problems and using numbers to find solutions. 我最喜欢的科目是数学，因为我喜欢解决问题，并且通过数字找到解决方案。

"时间"读法	
分类	举例
1. 整点读法：数字+o'clock	9:00 nine o'clock
2. 直接读法：按顺序读	9:07/ 8:10 nine o seven/ eight ten
3. 使用past/ to	30分钟以内 ... past ...	10:06 ten past six
	30分钟时 half past ...	11:30 half past eleven
	30分钟以后 ... to ...	8:45 a quarter to nine或fifteen to nine

"学校和科目" 问答常用词			
课程	相关形容词	相关动词	相关名词
maths 数学	interesting 有趣的	attend 参加	school 学校
English 英语	happy 高兴的	complete 完成	classroom 教室
Chinese 语文	useful 有用的	enter 进入	grade 年级
science 科学	boring 无聊的	finish 完成	class 班级
history 历史	difficult 困难的	learn 学习	course 课程
geography 地理	easy 容易的	study 学习	exam 考试
music 音乐	sad 悲伤的	dream 梦想	homework 家庭作业
PE 体育	dull 无趣的		lesson 课
art 美术			subject 科目

★必会句型★

1. 介绍所在学校、年级、班级

1) I am studying at ... Primary School. 我在……小学读书。

2) I am in Grade ... 我在……年级。

3) I am in Class ... 我在……班。

4) There are... students in our class. 我们班有……学生。

5) There are... girls in our class. 我们班有……女生。

6) There are... boys in our class. 我们班有……男生。

2. 介绍学校学习

1) I go to school at ... o'clock every day. 我每天……点去上学。

2) I come home from school at ... o'clock in the afternoon every day. 我每天下午……点放学回家。

3) My first lesson starts at ... 我的第一节课……点开始。

4) I have ... lessons three times a week. 我一周上三次……课。

5) I have ... minutes of sports in school. 我在学校有……分钟的体育活动时间。

6) I often finish my homework by myself. 我经常独立完成作业。

3. 介绍喜欢的科目

1) My favourite subject is... because... 我最喜欢的科目是……因为……

2) ... is interesting. ……很有趣。

3) I find it enjoyable and interesting. 我发现它令人愉快且有趣。

4) I love learning new words and improving my vocabularies. 我喜欢学习新单词，扩大我的词汇。

5) I enjoy solving problems and using numbers to find solutions. 我喜欢解决问题，并且通过数字找到解决方案。

Day 5 服装

 考场模拟

 Now, let's talk about **clothes**.
What clothes do you wear to school?

I usually wear the school uniform to school.

🎏 思路点拨

Q: **What clothes do you wear to school? 你上学穿什么衣服?**

I usually wear _____ to school.

我通常穿_____去上学。

*当被问到此类问题时，考生据实回答即可，如wear the school uniform（穿校服）。

🔔 考点锦囊

"服装颜色" 常见问答	
Q我是考官	A我是考生
What's your favourite colour for clothes? 你最喜欢什么颜色的衣服?	My favourite colour is blue. 我最喜欢的颜色是蓝色。
What colour is your coat? 你的外套是什么颜色的?	My coat is white. 我的外套是白色的。
What clothes do you wear when you go to a party? 你去参加聚会时穿什么衣服?	I usually wear a pretty dress. 我通常穿漂亮的连衣裙。
	I usually wear a nice jacket. 我通常穿一件漂亮的夹克。
What do you wear at school? 你在学校穿什么?	I usually wear my school uniform. 我通常穿校服。
Do you prefer to wear casual clothes or formal clothes? 你更喜欢穿休闲装还是正装?	I prefer to wear casual clothes. I feel comfortable when wearing casual clothes. 我更喜欢穿休闲装。我穿休闲服时感觉很舒服。

"旧衣物回收" 常见问答	
Q我是考官	A我是考生
What do you do with your old clothes? 你怎么处理你的旧衣服?	I don't throw my old clothes away. I give them to the community. The staff in the community can hand out my clothes to those in need. 我不会把旧衣服扔掉而是捐给社区。社区工作人员会把我的衣服分发给需要的人。

各种服装			
上衣	下装	鞋子	配饰
T-shirt T恤衫	jeans 牛仔裤	shoes 鞋子	scarf 围巾

续表

各种服装			
上衣	下装	鞋子	配饰
shirt 衬衫	trousers 裤子	sports shoes 运动鞋	hat 帽子
blouse 女士短上衣	pants 裤子	trainers 运动鞋	gloves 手套
suit 西服	tights 紧身裤	sandals 凉鞋	sunglasses 太阳眼镜
coat 外套	shorts 短裤	boots 靴子	glasses 眼镜
jacket 夹克	skirt 裙子		handbag 手提包
school uniform 校服	dress 连衣裙		bracelet 手链
sweater 毛衣	swimming costume 泳衣		earring 耳环
jumper 针织套衫			a pair of gloves 一副手套

描述颜色的形容词			
white 白色的	brown 棕色的	red 红色的	pink 粉色的
black 黑色的	golden 金色的	orange 橙色的	purple 紫色的
grey 灰色的	green 绿色的	yellow 黄色的	blue 蓝色的

★必会句型★

1. 介绍日常穿搭

1) I usually wear ... to school. 我通常穿……去上学。

2) I usually wear ... 我通常穿……

3) I prefer to wear ... 我更喜欢穿……

4) I feel comfortable when wearing ... 我穿……感觉很舒服。

2. 介绍衣物颜色

1) My favourite colour is ... 我最喜欢的颜色是……

2) My coat is ... 我的外套是……

3) My schoolbag is ... 我的书包是……

3. 介绍旧衣物回收

1) I don't throw my ... away. 我不会把……扔掉。

2) I will give ... to the community. 我会把……捐给社区。

3) They can hand out my ... to those in need. 他们会把我的……分发给需要的人。

Weekend 二 每周一练

I. 选一选，选出最合适的答语。

( ) 1. Q: How long have you studied English?

A) It will be cloudy tomorrow.

B) I like orange because it is juicy.

C) I have studied English for five years.

( ) 2. Q: What's the weather like today?

A) I'm good at English.

B) It is sunny today.

C) I usually walk to school.

( ) 3. Q: What colour is your schoolbag?

A) My schoolbag is blue.

B) I am in Grade Four.

C) English is difficult for me.

( ) 4. Q: Which school do you go to?

A) I came here by bike.

B) My favourite colour is green.

C) I'm studying at Experiment Primary School.

( ) 5. Q: How far is your home from your school?

A) It's ten minutes' drive.

B) I always walk to school.

C) My father drove me here.

( ) 6. Q: When do you go to school every day?

A) I get home at 5 o'clock in the afternoon.

B) I go to school at 7 o'clock every day.

C) I started learning English when I was five.

II. 读一读，圈出正确的单词。

1. Which grade are you *on / in*?

2. I usually *has / have* lunch at school.

3. I have a *lot / pair* of homework to do every day.

4. Can you finish your homework *by / on* yourself?

5. We have summer holidays *in / at* August.

6. Which foreign language is *spoken / speak* in your country?

7. It takes 30 *minute / minutes* to get to school.

8. I prefer to *wear / wears* casual clothes.

9. My first lesson starts *at / on* half past eight.

10. I like to *drink / drinking* orange juice.

III. 将左右两列的相应内容连线，构成完整的一句话。

1. My first lesson   A. the uniform to school.

2. I started   B. does all the cooking in my family.

3. My mom usually   C. starts at eight o'clock.

4. I usually wear   D. learning English when I was six.

5. I'm in   E. forty students in my class.

6. There are   F. Class One.

7. It takes   G. four times a week.

8. I have math lessons   H. about an hour to get there.

IV. 判断下面句子正误，如有错，请圈出并将正确形式写在下面的横线上。

1. People speaks Chinese in China.   □

_____

2. What kind of food does you like best?   □

_____

3. It takes me about twenty minute to get to school.   □

_____

4. What do you usually have for breakfast? ☐

_____

5. Which middle school do you wants to attend? ☐

_____

6. I go to school by a bus. ☐

_____

7. They costs 100 yuan. ☐

_____

8. I do my homework after school. ☐

_____

V. 连词成句。

1. class / Which / you / in / are /?

_____

2. to / school / close / My / my / is / house /.

_____

3. English / my / I / studying / at / am / school /.

_____

4. is / English / a bit / for / difficult / me /.

_____

5. I / wear / usually / dress / a /.

_____

6. Her / is / the / favourite / hamburger / food /.

_____

7. It / raining / outside / is /.

_____

8. I / breakfast / porridge / for / often / have /.

_____

VI. 模拟演练。

>>Activity 1

Examiner: Now, let's talk about **weather**.

How's the weather today?

Candidate A/B: 1. _____

Examiner: Will it be warm tomorrow?

Candidate A/B: 2. _____

Examiner: What do you usually do in warm days?

Candidate A/B: 3. _____

Examiner: Please tell me something about your favourite season.

Candidate A/B: 4. _____

>>Activity 2

Examiner: Now, let's talk about **school**.

Which school are you studying at?

Candidate A/B: 5. _____

Examiner: Which grade are you in?

Candidate A/B: 6. _____

Examiner: When do you go to school every day?

Candidate A/B: 7. _____

Examiner: Please tell me something about your favourite subject.

Candidate A/B: 8. _____

Week 4

Part 1 假期娱乐

			第4周目标		
考试模块	时间	话题	我是考官	我是考生	
Part 1 Phase 2 假期娱乐	Day 1	假期	Where do you usually go on holiday?	I usually... on holiday.	☐
	Day 2	交通	How do you usually go to school?	I usually go to school...	☐
	Day 3	购物	How much are your shoes?	They are...	☐
	Day 4	网络	What do you like doing most on the Internet?	I like... most.	☐
	Day 5	音乐	Do you like music?	Yes, I do. No, I don't.	☐
	Weekend	每周一练	每周基础知识练习		☐

 Day 1 假期

 考场模拟

Now, let's talk about **holiday**.

Where do you usually go on holiday?

I usually go abroad on holiday.

 思路点拨

Q: **Where do you usually go on holiday? 你通常去哪里度假?**

I usually _____ on holiday.

我通常在_____度假。

*地点类问题通常以where开头，询问考生去哪儿做什么、去哪儿玩什么等。当听到where开头的问题时，考生就要知道这是要回答地点了，比如at school、go abroad等。

 考点锦囊

"周末" 常见问答	
Q我是考官	A我是考生
When does the weekend start for you and your family? 你和家人什么时候开始过周末？	Our weekend starts on Saturday. 我们的周末从星期六开始。
What do you usually do at the weekend? 你周末通常做什么？	I usually play football at the weekend. 我周末通常踢足球。
What will you do next weekend? 下周末你要做什么？	I'm going to meet my friends next weekend. 下周末我要去见我的朋友。
Please tell me something about your last weekend. 请告诉我你上周末是怎么过的。	I had a wonderful trip last weekend. 上周末我有一个愉快的旅行。

"假期" 常见问答	
Q我是考官	A我是考生
Do you have school holidays in August? 你们学校八月份放假吗？	Yes, we have summer holidays in August. 是的，我们在八月放暑假。
What did you do last summer holiday? 去年暑假你做了什么？	I went to Summer Palace last summer holiday. 去年暑假我去了颐和园。
Where do you want to go on holiday? 你假期想去哪里？	I want to go to Australia on holiday. 我假期想去澳大利亚。

"旅行" 常见问答	
Q我是考官	A我是考生
What cities have you been to? 你去过哪些城市？	I have been to Beijing and Shanghai. 我去过北京和上海。

"旅行" 常见问答	
Q我是考官	A我是考生
Have you been to any other countries? 你去过其他国家吗？	Yes, I have been to Singapore. 是的，我去过新加坡。
How often do you travel to a foreign country? 你多久去一次国外？	I travel to a foreign country once a year. 我每年去国外旅行一次。
Do you think travelling can make you more knowledgeable? 你认为旅游能使你更有见识吗？	Yes, travelling can broaden my horizons. 是的，旅行可以开阔我的视野。
Do you like travelling? 你喜欢旅行吗？	Yes, I like travelling all over my country. 是的，我喜欢在全国各地旅游。

喜欢度假的原因	
have fun 玩得开心	see the world 看看世界
see animals 看看动物	explore nature 探索大自然
play on the beach 在海滩上玩	explore new places 探索新地方
visit museums 参观博物馆	learn about different cultures 了解不同文化
go on an adventure 冒险	broaden one's horizons 拓宽视野
eat new foods 吃新的食物	satisfy one's curiosity 满足好奇心
take photos 拍照	experience new things 体验新事物

度假必备		
backpack 背包	passport 护照	camera 相机
booklet 小册子	visa 签证	phone 手机
luggage 行李	ticket 机票	charger 充电器
suitcase 手提箱	map 地图	headphones 耳机
carry-on 随身携带的物品	guidebook 旅行指南	laptop 笔记本电脑

★必会句型★

1. 介绍周末活动

1) I usually ... at the weekend. 我周末通常……

2) I had a wonderful trip last weekend. 上周末我有一个愉快的旅行。

3) I'm going to ... next weekend. 下周末我要……

4) Our weekend starts on ... 我们的周末从……开始。

2. 介绍暑假寒假

1) We have summer holidays in August. 我们在八月放暑假。

2) I went to ... last winter holiday. 去年寒假我去了……

3) I want to go to ... on holiday. 我假期想去……

3. 介绍旅行度假

1) I have been to ... 我去过……

2) I travel to ... once a year. 我每年去……旅行一次。

3) I usually travel by ... 我通常乘……旅行。

4) I like travelling all over my country. 我喜欢在全国各地旅游。

5) Travelling can broaden my horizons. 旅行可以开阔我的视野。

Day 2 交通

 考场模拟

Now, let's talk about **traffic.**

How do you usually go to school?

I usually go to school on foot.

 思路点拨

Q: **How do you usually go to school? 你通常怎么去上学?**

I usually go to school _____.

我通常_____去上学。

*how意为"怎样",可以用来询问方式、方法等,如How do you usually go to school? 回答时可用"坐地铁""步行"等。

考点锦囊

\"日常交通\"常见问答	
Q我是考官	A我是考生
How do you get to school every day? 你每天怎么去学校?	I usually **walk to school**. 我通常步行去学校。
How far is your home from your school? 你家离学校有多远?	It's **about ten minutes' walk**. 步行大约需要十分钟。
How long does it take you to get to school? 你到学校要用多长时间?	It takes me **about twenty minutes** to get to school. 我到学校大约需要二十分钟。
How did you get here this morning? 你今天早上是怎么来的?	My father **drove me** here. 我爸爸开车送我来的。
How does your mother go to work? 你妈妈怎么去上班?	My mother goes to work **by car**. 我妈妈开车去上班。

\"旅行交通\"常见问答	
Q我是考官	A我是考生
How do you like to travel if you are going on a long journey? 如果长途旅行的话，你喜欢怎样旅行?	If I'm going on a long journey, I like to travel **by train**. 如果长途旅行的话，我喜欢乘火车旅行。
How do you usually travel? 你通常怎么旅行?	I usually travel **by plane**. 我通常乘飞机旅行。
	I usually travel with my parents. We like to take a tour with a caravan. 我通常跟父母一起旅行。我们喜欢开房车旅行。
When was the first time you took a train? 你第一次坐火车是什么时候?	The first time I took a train was **when I was six years old**. 我第一次坐火车是在我六岁的时候。
Do you like travelling by train? 你喜欢乘火车旅行吗?	**Yes**, I like travelling by train. 是的，我喜欢乘火车旅行。
Do you prefer taking a bus or the subway? 你更喜欢坐公共汽车还是地铁?	I prefer **taking the subway**. 我更喜欢乘地铁。

\"交通\"高阶问答	
Q我是考官	A我是考生
Do you think people will drive more in the future? 你认为未来人们会更多地开车吗?	**No**, I don't think so. **Actually** I suppose people will drive less in the future **because** the traffic condition is very horrible today. 不，我不这样认为。事实上，我想人们将来会减少开车，因为现在的交通状况非常糟糕。

"交通"高阶问答	
Q我是考官	A我是考生
Please tell me something about how you travelled to school yesterday. 请告诉我你昨天是怎么去学校的。	I took the subway to school yesterday. It just took fifteen minutes. I arrived at school on time. 我昨天乘地铁去学校。只花了15分钟。我准时到达学校。

"交通方式"常用表达		
介词表达	take + 冠词 + 交通工具	动词+to+地点/副词
on foot 步行	take a bus 乘公交车	walk to school 步行去学校
by bike 骑自行车	take a taxi 乘出租车	ride to school 骑车去学校
by bus 乘公共汽车	take a train 坐火车	drive to Shanghai 开车去上海
by subway 坐地铁	take a ship 坐船	drive home 开车回家
by car 乘小汽车	take a caravan 坐房车	fly to Guangzhou 乘飞机去广州
by train 坐火车		
by plane 坐飞机		
by boat 坐船		

★必会句型★

1. 介绍日常通勤

1) I usually ... to school. 我通常……去学校。

2) It's about ... minutes' walk. 步行大约需要……分钟。

3) It takes me about ... to get to school. 我花了大约……到学校。

4) ... drove me here. ……开车送我来的。

5) My mother goes to work by ... 我妈妈乘……去上班。

2. 介绍交通出行

1) If I'm going on a long journey, I like to travel by ... 如果长途旅行的话，我喜欢乘……旅行。

2) The first time I took a ... was when I was ... years old. 我第一次坐……是在我……岁的时候。

3) I like travelling by ... 我喜欢乘坐……旅行。

4) I prefer taking ... 我更喜欢乘坐……

3. 介绍交通情况

1) The traffic condition is ... today. 现在的交通状况……

2) Actually I suppose people will ... because ... 事实上，我想人们将来会……，因为……

Day 3　购物

考场模拟

Now, let's talk about **shopping**.

How much are your shoes?

They are about 300 yuan.

思路点拨

Q: **How much are your shoes?** 你的鞋子多少钱?

They are _____.

它们是_____。

*how much对"价格"提问，回答时用复数代词they指代your shoes，后用be动词are，完整句型为They are+价格。如100元，即They are one hundred yuan.

考点锦囊

"购物"常见问答	
Q我是考官	A我是考生
How often do you go shopping? 你多久购物一次?	I go shopping once a month. 我每月购物一次。
Do you like buying clothes? 你喜欢买衣服吗?	Yes, I like buying clothes, especially beautiful dresses. 是的，我喜欢买衣服，尤其是漂亮的连衣裙。
	No, my mum does. She always buys nice clothes for me. 不，我妈妈喜欢买衣服。她总是给我买好看的衣服。

"购物"常见问答	
Q我是考官	A我是考生
Are there many shops around your house? 你家附近有很多商店吗？	**Yes**, there are many shops around my house. 是的，我家附近有很多商店。
Do you prefer to go shopping by yourself or with your friends? 你更喜欢自己去购物还是和朋友一起去？	I prefer to go shopping **with my friends**. 我更喜欢跟朋友一起去购物。

"购物"高阶问答	
Q我是考官	A我是考生
Do you prefer online shopping or in-store shopping? Why? 你更喜欢在网上购物还是去实体店购物？为什么？	I prefer **in-store shopping because** it can provide the **real item** I want to buy. 我更喜欢在实体店购物，因为实体店可以提供我想买的实物。
Do you think shopping can be fun? 你认为购物很有趣吗？	**Yes**, I do. I **feel relaxed** during shopping. 是的，购物时我感觉很放松。
Do you think online shopping will replace traditional shopping? 你认为网上购物会取代传统购物吗？	Yes, I think so. Online shopping is **so easy and convenient that** more and more people shop online. 我想是的。网上购物非常便捷，越来越多的人在网上购物。

购买物品		
toy 玩具	book 书	drawing tools 绘画工具
soft toy 毛绒玩具	diary 日记本	eraser 橡皮擦
puzzle 拼图	notebook 笔记本	ruler 尺子
sticker 贴纸	pencil case 铅笔盒	pen 钢笔
ball 球	pencils 铅笔	

★必会句型★

1. 介绍购物习惯

1) I go shopping once a month. 我每月购物一次。

2) I like buying ..., especially ... 我喜欢买……，尤其是……

3) I prefer to go shopping ... 我更喜欢……去购物。

4) There are many ... shops around my house. 我家附近有很多……店。

2. 介绍购物方式

1) I prefer ... because ... 我更喜欢……，因为……

2) In-store shopping can provide ... 实体店可以提供……

3) Online shopping is so ... that more and more people ... 网上购物是如此的……以至于越来越多的人……

3. 介绍购物感受

I feel ... during shopping. 购物时我感觉……

Day 4　网络

 考场模拟

Now, let's talk about **Internet**.

What do you like doing most on the Internet?

I like chatting online most.

 思路点拨

Q: **What do you like doing most on the Internet?** 你最喜欢在网上做什么？

I like ＿＿＿＿＿＿＿＿＿＿＿ most.

我最喜欢＿＿＿＿＿＿＿＿＿＿＿。

*what意为"什么"。对于what开头的喜好类问题，回答时常用到I like/ love...（我喜欢……）、I like... most/ best...（我最喜欢……）或My favourite... is...（我最喜欢的……是……）。

考点锦囊

"网络"常见问答	
Q我是考官	A我是考生
How often do you chat online with your friends? 你多久和朋友网聊一次?	I chat online with my friends three times a week. 我每周和朋友网聊三次。
How often do you watch a movie on the Internet? 你多久在网上看一次电影?	I watch a movie on the Internet once a month. 我每月在网上看一次电影。
Which online programmes do you like best? Why? 你最喜欢哪个线上节目? 为什么?	My favourite online programme is the cartoon. It is very funny. 我最喜欢的线上节目是卡通片。它很有趣。
	I like basketball matches best because it makes me happy. 我最喜欢篮球比赛,因为它使我快乐。
Who uses the Internet most in your family? 你家谁最常上网?	My father uses the Internet most. He has a lot of work to do on the Internet. 我爸爸使用互联网最多。他有很多工作要在网上做。
What can you do on the Internet? 你上网做什么?	I can watch funny videos on the Internet. 我在网上看搞笑视频。
	I sometimes have online courses on the Internet, sometimes play online games with my friends. 我有时候在网上上网课,有时候跟朋友一起玩网络游戏。
How many hours a day do you use the Internet? 你每天上网几个小时?	I surf the Internet for half an hour every day. 我每天上网半小时。

上网活动	
learn online 在线学习	listen to music online 在线听音乐
play online games 玩网络游戏	read books online 在线看书
watch videos online 在线看视频	download files 下载文件
chat online 在线聊天	surf the Internet 上网冲浪
chat with friends online 与朋友在线聊天	search the web 搜索网页

★必会句型★

1. 介绍上网频次

1) I chat online with my friends three times a week. 我每周和朋友在线聊天三次。

2) I ... on the Internet once a week. 我每周一次在网上……

3) I surf the Internet for... every day. 我每天上网……

4) ... uses the Internet most. ……使用互联网最多。

5) He has a lot of ... to do on the Internet. 他在网上有很多……要做。

2. 介绍线上活动

1) My favourite online programme is ... 我最喜欢的线上节目是……

2) I can watch ... on the Internet. 我在网上看……

3) I sometimes ... on the Internet, sometimes ... with my friends. 我有时候在网上……，有时候跟朋友一起……

Day 5 音乐

 考场模拟

 Now, let's talk about **music**.

Do you like music?

Yes, I do. I like pop music very much.

 思路点拨

Q: **Do you like music? 你喜欢音乐吗?**

Yes, I do. I like _____.

是的，我喜欢_____。

*无论是肯定回答还是否定回答，都不要只说一个词，建议说完整句子。此外，还可以补充一些细节，比如你最喜欢什么类型的音乐、喜欢什么时候听音乐等。

Week 4

 考点锦囊

"音乐"常见问答	
Q我是考官	A我是考生
How often do you listen to music? 你多久听一次音乐？	I listen to music **not very often**. 我不常听音乐。
	I listen to music **every day**. 我每天都听音乐。
Can you play a musical instrument? 你会演奏乐器吗？	**Yes**, I can play the violin. 是的，我会拉小提琴。
	No, I can't play any musical instruments yet. But I always want to learn to play the guitar. 不，我现在还不会任何乐器，但我一直想学弹吉他。
Have you ever been to a concert? 你去过音乐会吗？	**No**, I have never been to a concert yet. 不，我还从来没去过音乐会。

"音乐"高阶问答	
Q我是考官	A我是考生
What kind of music do you think is suitable for children? 你认为什么样的音乐适合孩子们听？	I think **simple and happy music** is suitable for children **because** they can sing and dance with the music. 我认为简单快乐的音乐适合孩子，因为孩子们可以跟着音乐唱歌跳舞。
Do you prefer to listen to the background music in the shopping malls and shops or not? Why? 你喜不喜欢在商场和商店里听背景音乐？为什么？	**No**, I don't. The background music can be too loud and make it hard for me to hear and communicate with others. 不，我不喜欢。背景音乐可能太吵，让我很难听到并与他人交流。
Do you think music is important? Why? 你认为音乐重要吗？为什么？	**Yes**, I do. Music can convey messages, express emotions, and bring people together. 是的，我认为音乐很重要。音乐可以传达信息、表达情感，并将人们聚集在一起。

音乐类型	
classical music 古典音乐	rock music 摇滚音乐
pop music 流行音乐	hip hop music 嘻哈音乐
light music 轻音乐	jazz music 爵士音乐
country music 乡村音乐	R&B (rhythm and blues) 节奏布鲁斯

喜欢音乐的原因	
like the rhythm 喜欢节奏	like this singer 喜欢这个歌手
love the lyrics 喜欢歌词	like the band 喜欢这个乐队
enjoy the melody 喜欢旋律	want to dance to the beat 想跟着节奏跳舞
enjoy the music video 喜欢音乐视频	like the instruments 喜欢乐器

★必会句型★

1. 介绍音乐相关的爱好

1) I listen to music not very often. 我不常听音乐。

2) I can play the ... 我会弹……

3) I have never been to ... yet. 我还从来没去过……

2. 介绍音乐的影响

1) Simple and happy music is suitable for ... 简单快乐的音乐适合……

2) Children can ... with the music. 孩子们可以跟着音乐……

3) I think ... music is ... 我认为……音乐是……

3. 介绍音乐的魅力

Music can convey messages, express emotions, and bring people together. 音乐可以传达信息、表达情感，并将人们聚集在一起。

Weekend 三 每周一练

I. 选一选，选出最合适的答语。

( ) 1. Q: What did you do last summer holiday?

A) I usually walk to school.

B) I like to go shopping with my friends.

C) I went to Shanghai last summer holiday.

( ) 2. Q: Do you prefer taking a bus or the subway?

A) I use the Internet to do my homework.

B) I prefer taking the subway.

C) I usually go abroad on holiday.

(　) 3.　Q: How much is your shirt?

　　　A) I can play the piano

　　　B) It cost me about 200 yuan.

　　　C) My father drove me here.

(　) 4.　Q: Did you go on holiday last year?

　　　A) I plan to go to the library this Sunday.

　　　B) I have been to Beijing and Shanghai.

　　　C) Yes, I did. I went to Europe.

(　) 5.　Q: How often do you listen to music?

　　　A) I listen to music every day.

　　　B) I watch online videos twice a week.

　　　C) I have been to Beijing.

(　) 6.　Q: How does your mother go to work?

　　　A) He usually rides to school.

　　　B) I came here by bike.

　　　C) She goes to work by car.

II. 读一读，圈出正确的单词。

1. I'm going to *meet / meets* my friends next weekend.

2. My family is *going / go* to the Great Wall this summer.

3. We went there by plane and enjoyed *ourselves / ourself*.

4. I like long journeys by *plane / planes*.

5. How *did / do* you get here this morning?

6. I had *a / an* wonderful trip last weekend.

7. I take a *bus / buses* to school every day.

8. It depends *on / at* my parents' time.

9. How often *did / do* you go shopping?

10.　I *am / is* a big fan of music.

III. 将左右两列的相应内容连线，构成完整的一句话。

1. I like   A. colour is white.

2. My parents   B. walks to school.

3. She often   C. use the Internet most.

4. My favourite   D. classical music very much.

5. There are many clothes shops   E. the Internet for an hour every day.

6. Our weekend   F. shopping by myself.

7. I surf   G. around my house.

8. I prefer to go   H. starts on Saturday.

IV. 判断下面句子正误，如有错，请圈出并将正确形式写在下面的横线上。

1. Can you play a violin?   ☐
   _____

2. I can learns English on the Internet.   ☐
   _____

3. I had wonderful trip last weekend.   ☐
   _____

4. I like to go shopping by myself.   ☐
   _____

5. What do you like to do most on the Internet?   ☐
   _____

6. What kinds of music do you like best?   ☐
   _____

7. I have been to Hainan last years.   ☐
   _____

8. Who are your favourite singer?   ☐
   _____

V. 连词成句。

1. shopping / I / online / like /.

_____

2. you / Have / ever / to / been / concert / a /?

_____

3. I / go / usually / to / foot / school / on /.

_____

4. How / is / your / much / T-shirt /?

_____

5. musical / Can / you / a / instrument / play /?

_____

6. How / travelling / do / usually / go / you /?

_____

7. I / with / friends / my / online / chat /.

_____

8. any / Do / plans / you / for / this / have / Sunday /?

_____

VI. 模拟演练。

>>Activity 1

Examiner:	Now, let's talk about **holiday**.
	Do you have school holidays in August?
Candidate A/B: 1.	_____
Examiner:	Where do you want to go on holiday?
Candidate A/B: 2.	_____
Examiner:	Have you ever been to any other countries?
Candidate A/B: 3.	_____
Examiner:	Please tell me something about your last holiday.
Candidate A/B: 4.	_____

>>Activity 2

Examiner:	Now, let's talk about **music**.
	Do you like music?
Candidate A/B:	5. _____
Examiner:	How often do you listen to music?
Candidate A/B:	6. _____
Examiner:	What kind of music do you think is popular?
Candidate A/B:	7. _____
Examiner:	Please tell me something about your favourite singer.
Candidate A/B:	8. _____

Week

5

Part 2 人物介绍

考试模块	时间	话题	我是考官	我是考生	
			第5周目标		
Part 2 人物介绍	Day 1	人物描述	Please tell me something about your best friend.	My best friend is... He/ she is...	☐
	Day 2	家庭生活	Who does the housework in your family?	My mother does most of the housework such as...	☐
	Day 3	兴趣爱好	Do you like reading?	Yes, I like... Reading can...	☐
	Day 4	体育运动	What's your favourite sport?	I like... very much and I can...	☐
	Day 5	社会交往	When was the last time you shouted at your sister?	I remembered...	☐
	Weekend	每周一练	每周基础知识练习		☐

Day 1 人物描述

  考场模拟

Please tell me something about your best friend.

My best friend is Qiqi. She is my classmate. She is nice and friendly. We have known each other for many years. We often play together.

思路点拨

Q: **Please tell me something about your best friend. 请你跟我说说你最好的朋友。**

My best friend is_____. He/ she is _____.

我最好的朋友是_____。他/她是_____。

*Please tell me something about... （请告诉我一些关于……），属于描述类问题，考生需用2～5句话介绍。描述人物可以从外貌、职业、爱好、相处如何等角度阐述。

 考点锦囊

"人物描述" 常见问答	
Q我是考官	A我是考生
Who is your best friend? 你最好的朋友是谁?	My best friend is Li Mei. 我最好的朋友是李梅。
What does she look like? 她长什么样子?	She has long hair and she looks very nice. 她有一头长发，她看起来很漂亮。
Who is your favourite singer? Why? 你最喜欢的歌手是谁? 为什么?	My favourite singer is Eason Chan. I think he is very cool. My favourite song is his *Lonely Warrior*. 我最喜欢的歌手是陈奕迅。我觉得他很酷。我最喜欢的歌是他的《孤勇者》。

"人物描述" 高阶问答	
Q我是考官	A我是考生
Please tell me something about your family. 请告诉我一些关于你家人的事情。	There are three people in my family. They are my parents and me. My mother is a teacher, and my father works in a hospital. I love my family. 我家有三口人，分别是我的爸爸、妈妈和我。我妈妈是老师，我爸爸在医院工作。我爱我的家人。

关系	外貌	性格	职业
family 家人	long hair 长头发	kind 和蔼的	teacher 老师
classmate 同学	short hair 短头发	nice 亲切的	doctor 医生
friend 朋友	blond(e) 金发的	friendly 友好的	engineer 工程师
teammate 队友	curly 卷曲的	honest 诚实的	artist 艺术家
relative 亲戚	tall（个子）高的	serious 严肃的	police 警察
grandparents 祖父母	short（个子）矮的	polite 有礼貌的	lawyer 律师
grandpa 爷爷	strong 健壮的	gentle 和蔼友善的	manager 经理
grandma 奶奶	thin 瘦的	lovely 可爱的	designer 设计师

续表

关系	外貌	性格	职业
aunt 姑，姨	wear glasses 戴眼镜	naughty 淘气的	editor 编辑
uncle 叔，舅	beard 胡须	strict 严格的	driver 司机
cousin 表亲，堂亲	good-looking 好看的	hardworking 努力的	scientist 科学家
	beautiful 美丽的	cheerful 高兴的	pilot 飞行员
	handsome 英俊的	shy 害羞的	
	pretty 漂亮的	helpful 愿意帮忙的	

★必会句型★

1. 介绍好朋友外貌、日常相处等

1) My best friend is ... 我最好的朋友是······

2) She has ...hair. 她有一头······发。

3) She looks ... 她看起来······

4) He is ... 他是······

5) We have known each other for many years. 我们已经认识很多年了。

6) We often play together. 我们经常一起玩。

2. 介绍家人职业、性格等

1) My mother is ... 我妈妈是······

2) My father works in ... 我爸爸在······工作。

Day 2　家庭生活

 考场模拟

　Who does the housework in your family?

My mother does most of the housework such as cleaning the room and washing the clothes.

🎒 思路点拨

Q: **Who does the housework in your family? 你家谁做家务？**

My mother does most of the housework such as _____.

我妈妈做大部分的家务，比如_____。

*who意为"谁"。人员类问题一般会询问家里谁做某事、最喜欢的明星是谁、最好的朋友是谁等，回答时要用完整的句子，不要只说人名，比如，My mother does most of the housework.（我妈妈做了大部分的家务。）此外，考生可以通过补充细节、举例、引申来丰富答语，比如用such as或for example引出例子，such as cleaning the room and washing the clothes（比如打扫房间和洗衣服）。

考点锦囊

"家庭生活"常见问答	
Q我是考官	A我是考生
Who washes the dishes in your family? 你家谁负责洗碗?	My mum or my dad. It depends on their time. 我妈妈或者我爸爸。这取决于他们的时间。
Who cooks food in your family? 你们家谁做饭?	My mum usually does all the cooking in my family. 我家通常是我妈妈做饭。
Can you cook at home? 你会在家做饭吗?	Yes, I can make fried eggs. 是的，我会做煎蛋。
How often do you visit/ see your grandparents? 你多久看望你的祖父母一次?	I visit/ see my grandparents once a month. 我每月看望我的爷爷奶奶一次。

"频率"相关表达	
方法	示例
1. every+时间词	every day 每天
	every week 每周
	every month 每月
	every year 每年
2. 频率副词+时间词（a week/ month/ year）	once a week 每周一次
	twice a month 每月两次
	three times a year 每年三次

"家庭生活" 高阶问答	
Q我是考官	A我是考生
Please tell me something about your family. 请告诉我一些关于你家人的事情。	My family is a happy one. There are three members in my family, my father, mother, and me. My parents love me very much and I love them as well. 我的家庭是一个幸福的家庭。我家有三口人，爸爸、妈妈和我。我的父母很爱我，我也很爱他们。
Please tell me something about how your family spend time together on special occasions. 请告诉我你的家人是如何在特殊场合共度时光的。	On my last birthday I went to the beach with my family. We played on the beach and swam in the sea. It was a good day. 去年我生日的那天，我和家人去了海滩。我们在沙滩上玩耍，在海里游泳。那是美好的一天。

家务劳动		
make a bed 整理床铺	wash the dishes 洗碗	wash clothes 洗衣服
clean the room 打扫房间	do the cooking 做饭	do the laundry 洗衣服
clean the windows 擦窗户	cook the meal 做饭	hang out the clothes 晒衣服
clean the floor 擦地板	make dinner 做晚餐	fold clothes 叠衣服
sweep the floor 清扫地板	water the flowers 浇花	feed the pet 喂宠物
clean the yard 打扫院子	wash the car 洗车	

★必会句型★

1. 介绍家庭劳动

1) I can ... 我会做……

2) ... usually does all the cooking in my family. 我家通常是……做饭。

3) ... washes the dishes in my family. 在我家，……洗碗。

2. 介绍探望长辈

1) I visit my grandparents once a month. 我每月看望我的祖父母一次。

2) Last week, I visited my ... 上周，我去看望了我的……

3. 介绍生日聚会

1) On my last birthday I went to ... with my family. 去年我生日的那天，我和家人去了……

2) It was a good day. 那是美好的一天。

Day 3 兴趣爱好

 考场模拟

> Do you like reading?

> Yes, I like reading very much. Reading can broaden my horizons and I especially like reading books about history.

 思路点拨

Q: **Do you like reading? 你喜欢阅读吗？**

Yes, I like reading. Reading can _____.

是的，我喜欢阅读。阅读可以_____。

*考生可根据实际情况作答，建议给出原因或者引申内容。

 考点锦囊

"兴趣爱好"常见问答	
Q我是考官	A我是考生
Do you like listening to music? 你喜欢听音乐吗？	**Yes**, I do. I've downloaded several music apps. 是的，我喜欢听音乐。我下载了几个音乐app。
Do you think drawing is difficult? 你觉得画画难吗？	**No**, I like drawing. I can draw quite well. 不，我喜欢画画。我画得很好。
Do you think reading is fun? 你认为阅读有趣吗？	**Yes**, I think so. Reading can help us relax. 是的，我认为阅读很有趣。阅读可以帮助我们放松。
Do you think playing an instrument is fun? 你觉得演奏乐器有趣吗？	Sure. I like playing the piano very much. 当然啦。我非常喜欢弹钢琴。
What kind of things do you like reading? 你喜欢读什么样的书？	I like reading books about nature. This kind of books makes me learn about the natural world. 我喜欢读关于自然的书。这类书使我了解自然界。

续表

"兴趣爱好" 常见问答	
Q我是考官	A我是考生
How often do you do your favourite hobby? 你多久进行一次你最喜欢的爱好?	I do my favourite hobby three times a week. 我每周做三次我最喜欢的爱好。
What do you usually do in your spare time? 你在闲暇时间通常做什么呢?	I usually play badminton with my friends. It is of great fun to play badminton. 我通常和朋友打羽毛球。打羽毛球很有趣。

"兴趣爱好" 高阶问答	
Q我是考官	A我是考生
Which is more interesting, playing computer games or listening to music? 玩电脑游戏和听音乐,哪个更有趣呢?	I think playing computer games is more interesting because when I listen to music, I always fall asleep. 我认为玩电脑游戏更有趣,因为当我听音乐时,我总是犯困。
Which is more fun, playing sports or watching sports? Why? 参加体育运动和观看体育比赛,哪个更有趣? 为什么?	I prefer to watch sports. I can see my favourite basketball stars on TV. When they win, I'll be very happy. 我更喜欢观看体育比赛。我可以在电视上看到我最喜欢的篮球明星。如果他们赢了,我会很高兴。

兴趣爱好(like/ love/ enjoy +doing)		
运动竞技类	乐器类	休闲娱乐类
jogging 慢跑	playing the drum 打鼓	watching TV 看电视
fishing 钓鱼	playing the guitar 弹吉他	playing computer games 玩电脑游戏
hiking 远足	playing the piano 弹钢琴	collecting stamps 集邮
climbing 爬山	playing the violin 拉小提琴	dancing 跳舞
skiing 滑雪	playing the flute 吹笛子	drawing(用铅笔或钢笔)绘画
swimming 游泳		painting(用颜料)绘画
playing cards 打牌		listening to music 听音乐
playing chess 下棋		singing 唱歌
playing board games 棋类游戏		camping 露营
		making puzzles 拼图游戏
		taking photographs 拍照
		cooking 烹饪
		reading 阅读

★必会句型★

1. 介绍兴趣爱好

1) I like ... 我喜欢……

2) I like ... very much. 我非常喜欢……

3) I can ... quite well. 我能……得很好。

4) I do my favourite hobby ... a week. 我每周做……次我最喜欢的爱好。

2. 介绍喜欢的原因

1) ... can help us relax. ……可以帮助我们放松。

2) I usually ... with my friend. 我通常和朋友一起……

3) It is of great fun to ... 做……很有趣。

4) I think ... is more interesting because ... 我认为……更有趣，因为……

5) I prefer to ... / I can ... 我更喜欢…… / 我可以……

Day 4　体育运动

 考场模拟

 What's your favourite sport?

I like tennis very much and I can play it well.

思路点拨

Q: What's your favourite sport? 你最喜欢的运动是什么？

I like _____ very much and I can _____.

我喜欢_____我可以_____。

*考生在回答what开头的喜好类问题时，不但要给出观点，还要给出原因或者进行解释，比如，I like tennis very much and I can play it well.

考点锦囊

"体育运动" 常见问答	
Q我是考官	A我是考生
Do you like swimming? Why? 你喜欢游泳吗？为什么？	I don't like swimming, because I'm afraid of water. 我不喜欢游泳，因为我怕水。
Do you like playing basketball? Why? 你喜欢打篮球吗？为什么？	Yes, I like playing basketball. It's very popular at my school. 是的，我喜欢打篮球。篮球在我们学校很受欢迎。
Do you like cycling? Why? 你喜欢骑自行车吗？为什么？	Of course. I like cycling. It makes me keep fit. 当然啦。我喜欢骑自行车。骑行可以使我保持健康。
What position do you play? 你打什么位置？	It depends on the sports events I take part in. For example, I play the goalkeeper in the football game. 这取决于我参加的体育项目。比如，在足球比赛中我是守门员。
How can sports help you make friends? Why? 运动如何帮助你交朋友？为什么？	I play basketball with my classmates. We're a close team and we share everything about basketball: sports skills, favourite stars etc. 我和我的同学打篮球。我们是一支亲密无间的球队，我们分享关于篮球的一切：篮球技巧、最喜欢的明星等。

"体育运动" 高阶问答	
Q我是考官	A我是考生
Which of these sports events: football, basketball, volleyball, etc. do you play best? 足球、篮球、排球等运动中，你最擅长哪一项？	I can play volleyball very well. I started to play it when I was very young. 我排球打得很好。我在很小的时候就开始打排球。
Which sports is most fun to watch on television? Why? 在电视上观看什么运动最有趣？为什么？	Watching football matches is most fun. Football is my favourite sport. I often watch football matches on TV with my dad. 观看足球比赛最有趣。足球是我最喜欢的运动。我经常和爸爸在电视上看足球赛。
Which is more important, winning or losing in sports? 在体育运动中，输和赢哪个更重要？	I think winning is more important. Everybody wants to win the game and nobody wants to lose. 我认为赢更重要。每个人都想赢得比赛，没有人想输。
	In sports, the most important thing is to have fun and do my best, whether I win or lose. 在体育运动中，最重要的是玩得开心，尽我最大的努力，不管我是赢是输。

体育运动		
球类	田径	其他
baseball 棒球	run 跑步	skating 滑冰
basketball 篮球	marathon 马拉松赛跑	horse riding 骑马
hockey 曲棍球	jogging 慢跑	dive 潜水
ice-hockey 冰上曲棍球	jump 跳跃	boxing 拳击
football 足球	high jump 跳高	ski 滑雪
table tennis 乒乓球	long jump 跳远	skateboard 滑板
badminton 羽毛球		surfing 冲浪
volleyball 排球		
cricket 板球（运动）		

★必会句型★

1. 介绍喜欢、擅长的运动

1) I like ... It's ... 我喜欢……它……

2) I am good at ... 我擅长……

3) ... is my favourite sport. ……是我最喜欢的运动。

4) I started to ... when I was ... 当我……时就开始……

5) I don't like ..., because ... 我不喜欢……，因为……

2. 介绍"一项有趣的运动"

1) ... is more fun. ……更有趣。

2) I often watch ... matches on TV with my dad. 我经常和爸爸一起在电视上看……比赛。

3. 介绍"运动的益处"

1) ... makes me healthy. ……使我健康。

2) ... can help me make friends. ……能帮我交朋友。

3) We share everything about ... 我们分享关于……的一切。

4) It provides a common interest and a chance to work together as a team. 它提供了一个共同的兴趣和一个团队合作的机会。

4. 介绍"对输赢的看法"

1) I think ... is more important because ... 我认为……更重要，因为……

2) In sports, the most important thing is to ..., whether you win or lose. 在体育运动中，最重要的是……，不管你是赢是输。

 Day 5 社会交往

 考场模拟

> When was the last time you shouted at your sister?
>
> I remembered I shouted at my sister on Friday because she took my toy car away. I was very angry.

思路点拨

Q: **When was the last time you shouted at your sister? 你上次对妹妹大喊大叫是什么时候？**

I remembered ＿＿＿＿＿＿＿＿＿ because ＿＿＿＿＿＿＿＿＿.

我记得＿＿＿＿＿＿＿＿＿因为＿＿＿＿＿＿＿＿＿。

*when意为"什么时候"。以when开头的时间类问题，答语中常用到时间词，要注意介词的使用。在星期之前要用介词on，比如on Friday（在周五）。

 考点锦囊

"社会交往"常见问答	
Q我是考官	A我是考生
Do you have many friends? 你有很多朋友吗？	Yes, I have many friends. They are my classmates. 是的，我有很多朋友。他们是我的同学。
Do you like making friends? 你喜欢交朋友吗？	Sure, I like making friends. I made several friends in my drawing club. 当然，我喜欢交朋友。我在绘画社团里交了好几个朋友。
Do you have a penfriend? 你有笔友吗？	Yes, I have a pen pal. Her name is Lucy. 是的，我有一个笔友。她叫露西。

"社会交往" 常见问答	
Q我是考官	A我是考生
What do you usually chat about with your friends? 你通常和朋友聊什么?	I usually chat about my school life with my friends. We talk about the activities at school. 我经常和朋友聊校园生活。我们谈论校园活动。

"社会交往" 高阶问答	
Q我是考官	A我是考生
What do you have to do when you are asked to a party? 当你被邀请参加聚会时，你需要做什么?	When I am asked to a party, I need to reply and bring a gift to the party. 当我被邀请参加聚会时，我需要回复邀请并带礼物去聚会。
	When I am asked to a party, I need to decide whether to accept or decline the invitation. 当我被邀请参加聚会时，我需要决定是接受还是拒绝邀请。
	When I am asked to a party, firstly I need to know who will participate in the party. Secondly, I should make sure when and where the party will be held. 当我被邀请参加聚会时，首先我需要知道有哪些人参加这个聚会。其次，我应该确定聚会举行的时间和地点。
Do you think you can be a leader for a group of ten people? And Why? 你认为你能成为十人小组的领导吗? 为什么?	I think I can be a leader for a group of ten people because I am responsible, organized, and good at communicating with others. 我认为我可以成为一个十人团队的领导者，因为我有责任心、有组织能力，并且善于与他人沟通。
	I don't think so. It's a difficult job to be a leader. You have to be very skillful to communicate with so many people. I am not good at socializing with others. 我不这么认为。当领导是一项困难的工作。与人沟通需要很多技巧。我不善于与人交往。

社会交往		
greet 问候	make friends 交朋友	keep in touch 保持联系
talk 聊天	communicate 沟通	catch up 叙旧
introduce oneself 自我介绍	strike up a conversation 搭讪	go out together 一起出去
meet new people 认识新的人	chat with 与……聊天	socialize 社交
be friendly 友善	share things 分享东西	find common ground 找到共同点

★必会句型★

1. 与朋友相处

1) I have many friends. 我有很多朋友。

2) I like making friends. 我喜欢交朋友。

3) I have a pen pal. His / Her name is ... 我有一个笔友，他/她叫……

4) I usually chat about ... with ... 我经常和……聊……

5) We talk about ... 我们谈论……

2. 聚会邀请

1) I will accept the invitation. 我将接受这个邀请。

2) I will decline the invitation. 我将拒绝这个邀请。

3) When I am asked to a party, I need to... 当我被邀请参加聚会时，我需要……

4) I should bring a gift to the party. 我应该带一份礼物去聚会。

5) I should make sure when and where the party will be held. 我应该确定一下聚会举行的时间和地点。

3. 介绍社交情况

1) I am good at communicating with others. 我善于与他人沟通。

2) I prefer to work with other people. 我更喜欢与人共事。

3) I am responsible. 我有责任心。

4) When I work with others, I can ... 当我和别人一起工作时，我可以……

5) I am not good at socializing with others. 我不善于与人交往。

6) It's a difficult job to ... ……是一项困难的工作。

Weekend 二 每周一练

I. 选一选，选出最合适的答语。

( ) 1. Q: What does he look like?

A) I can do most of the housework.

B) He has short hair and wears glasses.

C) My mother is a lawyer.

( ) 2. Q: Do you like listening to music?

A) Yes, I have many music CDs.

B) My favourite dancer is Barbie.

C) About four times a week.

( ) 3. Q: Who do you often read books with?

A) I can play the piano.

B) I like playing basketball.

C) I often read books with my friends.

( ) 4. Q: How many hours do you do sports every day?

A) She is my classmate.

B) We often play together.

C) I do sports for an hour every day.

( ) 5. Q: Who does the housework in your family?

A) There are three people in my family.

B) I don't like swimming at all.

C) My mother does the housework.

( ) 6. Q: What do you like to do in your spare time?

A) I like to play volleyball with my friends.

B) I go to a park once a week.

C) I like pop music.

II. 读一读，圈出正确的单词。

1. I don't have *a / an* pen pal.

2. We often *chat / chatting* together.

3. Her name *is / are* Ann.

4. I like to go *swimming / swim* in summer.

5. She has long blond hair and *wear / wears* glasses.

6. I read *for / in* fun every day.

7. My father is an *engineers / engineer*.

8. I visit my grandparents every *weekend / weekends*.

9. My hobby is reading *because / so* reading is fun.

10. I go to the museum *once / one* a year.

III. 将左右两列的相应内容连线，构成完整的一句话。

1. I have   A. basketball with my classmates.

2. I play   B. the beach last summer.

3. I went to   C. looks very nice.

4. She   D. many friends.

5. He likes   E. to the cinema every week.

6. My favourite   F. together.

7. She goes   G. singer is King.

8. They often play   H. making friends.

IV. 判断下面句子正误，如有错，请圈出并将正确形式写在下面的横线上。

1. It's difficult job to be a leader. ☐

_____

2. What are your favourite sport? ☐

_____

3. I visit my uncle one a month. ☐

_____

4. There are three people in my family. ☐

_____

5. Can you play piano? ☐

_____

6. What often do you come here? ☐

_____

7. Do you like telling stories? ☐

_____

8. I usually helps my mom to do the housework. ☐

_____

V. 连词成句。

1. making / Do / like / you / friends /?

   _____

2. I / volleyball / young / started / when / I / to / play / very / was /.

   _____

3. home / you / at / cook / Can /?

   _____

4. round / has / a / She / face /.

   _____

5. Where / activities / your / do / do / you / favourite /?

   _____

6. What / like / does / look / he /?

   _____

7. We / years / have / each / known / other / for / many /.

   _____

8. I / animals / like / books / reading / about /.

   _____

VI. 模拟演练。

>>**Activity 1 Hobbies**

Examiner: Now, in this part of the test you are going to talk together. Here are some pictures that show **different hobbies**. Do you like these different hobbies? Say why or why not. I'll say that again. Do you like these different hobbies? Say why or why not. All right? Now, talk together.

Candidate A: Do you like drawing?

Candidate B: 1. _____

Examiner: Do you think drawing is fun?

Candidate A/B: 2. _____

Examiner: Do you think playing the guitar is boring?

Candidate A/B: 3. _____

Examiner: Which is more fun, playing the guitar or drawing?

Candidate A/B: 4. _____

Examiner: Thank you.

>>**Activity 2 Sports**

Examiner: Now, in this part of the test you are going to talk together. Here are some pictures that show **different sports**. Do you like these different sports? Say why or why not. I'll say that again. Do you like these different sports? Say why or why not. All right? Now, talk together.

Candidate B: Do you like playing table tennis?

Candidate A: 5. _____

Examiner: Do you think running is good for health?

Candidate A/B: 6. _____

Examiner: Do you think swimming is fun?

Candidate A/B: 7. _____

Examiner: Now, which is more important, winning or losing in sports?

Candidate A/ B: 8. _____

Examiner: Thank you.

Part 2 休闲活动

考试模块	时间	话题	我是考官	我是考生	
			第6周目标		
Part 2 休闲活动	Day 1	影视节目	What TV programme do you like best?	I like... best. It...	☐
	Day 2	动物宠物	Do you have pets?	Yes, I... She is... No, I don't... They are...	☐
	Day 3	传统节日	Which time of year is special in your country?	... is a special time in my country because...	☐
	Day 4	科学技术	What do you think smartphones can do nowadays?	I think...	☐
	Day 5	生活常识	How many seasons are there in a year in your country?	There are... They are...	☐
	Weekend	每周一练	每周基础知识练习		☐

Day 1　影视节目

 考场模拟

 What TV programme do you like best?

I like *Animal World* best. It makes me know more about the animals.

思路点拨

Q: **What TV programme do you like best?** 你最喜欢的电视节目是什么？

I like _____ best. It makes me _____.

我最喜欢_____。它让我_____。

*回答此类问题时，不仅要给出答案，还要给出相关理由。

考点锦囊

"影视节目" 常见问答	
Q我是考官	**A我是考生**
How often do you watch TV? 你多久看一次电视？	I watch TV only on weekends because I don't have too much time. 我只在周末看电视，因为我没有太多的时间。
When and where do you usually watch TV? 你通常什么时候在哪里看电视？	I usually watch TV in the living room on weekends. 我通常周末在客厅看电视。
How often do you go to the cinema? 你多久去一次电影院？	I usually go to the cinema once a month. 我通常每月去一次电影院。
What kind of movies do you like? 你喜欢什么类型的电影？	I prefer science fiction movies. They're interesting. 我更喜欢科幻电影。它们很有趣。
Do you like watching action films? 你喜欢看动作片吗？	No, I don't. I like cartoons because they are fun. 不，我不喜欢。我喜欢卡通片，因为它们很有趣。
What kind of things on TV makes you laugh? 电视上什么类型的内容能让你笑出声来？	Some talk shows can always make me laugh. 一些脱口秀节目总能让我开怀大笑。

"影视节目" 高阶问答	
Q我是考官	**A我是考生**
Please tell me something good that you watched on TV. 请告诉我一些你在电视上看过的好看的内容。	Sure! I recently watched a heartwarming movie called *The Secret Life of Pets*. It was really funny and made me laugh. 当然！我最近看了一部叫《爱宠大机密》的暖心电影。这真的很有趣，让我开怀大笑。
	Sure! Recently, I watched a really interesting wildlife documentary on TV. It was about different animals in their natural habitats. It was so interesting. 当然！最近，我在电视上看了一部非常有趣的野生动物纪录片。它是关于不同动物在自然栖息地的故事。太有趣了。

影视节目	
cartoons 动画片	news 新闻
animation 动画片	movie 电影
weather forecast 天气预报	football matches 足球比赛
Animal World《动物世界》	cooking shows 烹饪节目
reality shows 真人秀	programmes about history 历史节目
wildlife documentary 野生动物纪录片	a heartwarming movie 一部温暖人心的电影

喜欢某个节目的原因	
makes me laugh 让我大笑	interesting and engaging 有趣且引人入胜
so funny 很有趣	learn new things 学习新知识
so friendly and nice 非常友好和亲切	have a happy ending 有一个快乐的结局
so cool and interesting 很酷很有趣	a great way to pass the time and relax 消磨时间和放松的好方式

★必会句型★

1. 观影频率

1) I watch TV only on weekends because ... 我只在周末看电视，因为……

2) I usually go to the cinema once a month. 我通常每月去一次电影院。

2. 观影地点

I usually watch ... in the living room on weekends. 周末我通常在客厅里看……

3. 介绍喜欢的节目类型

1) I prefer the movies about ... They're interesting. 我更喜欢……类型的电影。它们很有趣。

2) I like ... because they're so exciting. 我喜欢……因为它们太令人兴奋了。

3) ... can always make me laugh. ……总能让我开怀大笑。

4. 介绍看过的令人印象深刻的节目

看了什么节目

I watched ... on TV last weekend. 上周末我在电视上看了……

I recently watched a heartwarming movie called ... 我最近看了一部叫……的暖心电影。

Recently, I watched a really ... on TV. 最近，我在电视上看了一部非常……

内容用1句话概括

It was about ... 它是关于……

It was the latest ... from my favourite ... 这是我最喜欢的……的最新……

喜欢的原因

I love..., and it's so beautiful. 我喜欢……，太美了。

It was so fascinating to learn about their ... 了解它们的……是非常有趣的。

It was really funny and made me smile all the time. 这真的很有趣，让我一直在笑。

Day 2　动物宠物

考场模拟

 Do you have pets?

Yes, I have a cat at home. She is quiet and lovely.

思路点拨

Q:　**Do you have pets? 你有养宠物吗？**

Yes, I ＿＿＿＿＿＿＿＿＿＿ . She is ＿＿＿＿＿＿＿＿＿＿ .

是的，我＿＿＿＿＿＿＿＿＿。她是＿＿＿＿＿＿＿＿＿。

/ No, I don't ＿＿＿＿＿＿＿＿＿ . They are ＿＿＿＿＿＿＿＿＿ .

/不，我不＿＿＿＿＿＿＿＿。他们是＿＿＿＿＿＿＿＿＿。

*考生不仅要回答yes/ no，还要给出一些补充细节，比如养了什么宠物、什么时候养的、为什么喜欢/ 不喜欢养宠物等。

考点锦囊

"动物"常见问答	
Q我是考官	A我是考生
Have you ever been to the zoo? 你曾经去过动物园吗？	Yes, I've been to the zoo when I was a little kid. 是的，我小时候去过动物园。

续表

"动物" 常见问答	
Q我是考官	A我是考生
What animals do you like? 你喜欢什么动物?	I like dogs. They are faithful to their masters. 我喜欢狗。它们对主人忠心耿耿。
Do you like animals? 你喜欢动物吗?	Yes, I like animals very much, especially pandas. They are so cute. 是的，我非常喜欢动物，尤其是熊猫。它们非常可爱。
How often do you go to the zoo? 你多久去一次动物园?	I go to the zoo once a year. 我每年去一次动物园。
Do you think zoos are exciting? 你认为动物园令人兴奋吗?	Yes, I think zoos are exciting because they allow us to see and learn about different types of animals in one place. 是的，我认为动物园是令人兴奋的，因为它们让我们在一个地方看到和了解不同类型的动物。
Do you think we human beings should take animals as our friends? 你认为人类应该把动物当作朋友吗?	Of course. We live in the same natural world, so we should live harmoniously with wild animals. 当然。我们生活在同一个自然世界，因此我们应该与野生动物和谐共处。
What animal would you like to be if you can choose? 如果能选择你想成为什么动物?	I want to be an elephant because it is strong and smart. 我想成为一头大象，因为它既强壮又聪明。

"宠物" 常见问答	
Q我是考官	A我是考生
What is your pet's name? 你的宠物叫什么?	My pet dog's name is Jimmy. 我的宠物狗的名字叫吉米。
How many pets have you had? 你养过多少只宠物?	I haven't had a pet ever. But I always hope I can keep a parrot one day. 我从来没有养过宠物。但是我一直希望有一天我能养一只鹦鹉。
Please tell me something about your pet. 请你跟我说说你的宠物。	My pet cat is very cute. It is always naughty. 我的宠物猫很可爱。它总是很淘气。
What animal do you think makes the best pet? 你认为什么动物是最好的宠物?	I think dogs are the best pet. They are man's best friends and they're friendly and cute. 我认为狗是最好的宠物。它们是人类最好的朋友，它们既友好又可爱。

"动物宠物" 高阶问答	
Q我是考官	A我是考生
Please tell me something about an animal that you like. 请告诉我你喜欢的一种动物。	My favourite animal is panda. I think panda is the cutest animal in the world. When I first saw pandas, I was so excited. 我最喜欢的动物是熊猫。我认为熊猫是世界上最可爱的动物。当我第一次看到熊猫时，我很兴奋。

续表

"动物宠物" 高阶问答	
Q我是考官	A我是考生
Please tell me something about your favourite pet. 请告诉我你最喜欢的一种宠物。	My favourite pet is **dog**. Her name is **Cindy**. She has **big eyes**. I like **playing with her**. 我最喜欢的宠物是狗。她的名字叫辛迪。她有一双大眼睛。我喜欢和她一起玩。

各种动物		
宠物	家畜	野生动物
bird 鸟	chicken 鸡	whale 鲸
parrot 鹦鹉	rooster 公鸡	dolphin 海豚
cat 猫	duck 鸭子	elephant 大象
kitten 小猫	pig 猪	tiger 老虎
dog 狗	sheep 绵羊	monkey 猴子
puppy 小狗	horse 马	giraffe 长颈鹿
fish 鱼		zebra 斑马
rabbit 兔子		

描述动物的形容词		
cute 可爱的	sweet 可爱的	small 小的
friendly 友好的	adorable 可爱的	big 大的
naughty 淘气的	fuzzy 毛茸茸的	tall 高大的
smart 聪明的	fluffy 毛茸茸的	short 矮小的
faithful 忠实的	furry 毛茸茸的	little 小小的
dangerous 危险的	fierce 凶猛的	wild 野生的

★必会句型★

1. 介绍 "喜欢的动物"

1) I like ... They are ... 我喜欢……它们……

2) My favourite animal is ... 我最喜欢的动物是……

3) I think ... 我觉得……

2. 介绍 "饲养的宠物"

1) My pet dog's name is ... 我的宠物狗的名字叫……

2) My pet cat is ... 我的宠物猫……

3) My favourite pet is ... 我最喜欢的宠物是……

4) Her name is ... 她的名字叫……

5) I like playing with her. 我喜欢和她一起玩。

3. 介绍"去动物园的时间及频率"

1) I've been to the zoo when ... 我……时候去过动物园。

2) I go to the zoo once a year. 我每年去一次动物园。

4. 介绍"对动物园和动物的看法"

1) I like to go to the zoo because there are lots of different animals in the zoo. 我喜欢去动物园，因为动物园里有许多不同的动物。

2) Animals are humans' friends. 动物是人类的朋友。

Day 3 传统节日

 考场模拟

Which time of year is special in your country?

Mid-Autumn Festival is a special time in my country because it is a time for family reunion.

思路点拨

Q: **Which time of year is special in your country?** 你们国家一年中的哪个时间是特别的？

_____ is a special time in my country because _____.

在我的国家，_____是个特别的日子，因为_____。

*which意为"哪一个""哪一些"，指在一定范围内的，比如which time of year（一年中的哪个时候）。考生在回答时除了要给出节日名，还要给出原因。

考点锦囊

"传统节日"常见问答	
Q我是考官	A我是考生
Is New Year a special time in your country? 在你们国家，新年是一个特殊的日子吗？	Yes, we celebrate New Year in my country. 是的，在我们国家我们庆祝新年。
Which festival do you like best? Why? 你最喜欢哪个节日？为什么？	I like the Mid-Autumn Festival best. We enjoy the moon while eating mooncakes. 我最喜欢中秋节。我们一边吃月饼一边赏月。

"传统节日"高阶问答	
Q我是考官	A我是考生
Please tell me something about the Spring Festival. 请告诉我一些关于春节的事情。	The Spring Festival is one of the most important festivals in China. It is very popular. All family members will get together on New Year's Eve and have a big meal. 春节是中国最重要的节日之一。它很受欢迎。所有的家庭成员会在除夕聚在一起吃一顿大餐。
Please tell me something about other traditional festivals in your country. 请告诉我一些你们国家的其他传统节日。	People in China celebrate the Dragon Boat Festival in memory of the great poet Qu Yuan. On that day, people eat rice dumplings and watch dragon boat races. 为了纪念伟大诗人屈原，中国人会庆祝端午节。在端午节，人们吃粽子、看龙舟赛。

传统节日	
Children's Day 儿童节（6月1日）	Double Ninth Festival 重阳节（农历九月初九）
Labour Day 劳动节（5月1日）	Dragon Boat Festival 端午节（农历五月初五）
New Year's Day 元旦（1月1日）	Mid-Autumn Festival 中秋节（农历八月十五）
National Day 国庆节（10月1日）	Lantern Festival 元宵节（农历正月十五）
Women's Day 妇女节（3月8日）	Spring Festival 春节（农历正月初一）
Teachers' Day 教师节（9月10日）	Tomb-sweeping Day 清明节（4月5日前后）

喜欢某个节日的原因	
have fun with friends 和朋友一起玩乐	eat delicious food 吃美味的食物
receive gifts and presents 收到礼物	eat mooncakes 吃月饼
get red packets from parents 从父母那里收红包	watch fireworks and displays 观看烟花表演
celebrate with family 和家人庆祝	wear beautiful clothes 穿漂亮的衣服

喜欢某个节日的原因	
get together with family 和家人团聚	have beautiful decorations 有漂亮的装饰
play and have fun 玩耍和找乐子	learn about Chinese culture and history 学习中国文化和历史

★必会句型★

1. 介绍喜欢的节日

1) I like ... best. We ... 我最喜欢……我们……

2) We celebrate ... in my country. 在我们国家，我们庆祝……

2. 介绍传统节日活动

1) ... is very popular. ……很受欢迎。

2) All family members will ... 所有的家庭成员会……

3) On that day, people ... 在那天，人们做……

4) The ... is one of the most important festivals in China. ……是中国最重要的节日之一。

5) ... is a special time in my country because ... ……是我国一个特殊的时间，因为……

6) People in China celebrate ... in memory of ... 为了纪念……，中国人会庆祝……

Day 4　科学技术

 考场模拟

 What do you think smartphones can do nowadays?

I think smartphones can do a lot of things. We can not only use smartphones to send text messages or make phone calls, but also use them to access Internet, shop online etc.

思路点拨

Q: **What do you think smartphones can do nowadays? 你认为现在智能手机能做什么？**

I think _____. We can not only use _____, but also _____.

我认为 _____。我们不仅可以使用 _____，还可以 _____。

*如果还没想到如何回答，这时一定不要沉默，什么都不说。你可以说：That's an interesting question...，用来争取思考的时间，然后再说出答案。

🔔 **考点锦囊**

"科学技术"问答	
Q我是考官	A我是考生
Do you think people still need to go to the offices since most of them do their work on computers? 大部分人用电脑工作，你认为他们还需要到办公室上班吗？	Yes, I think so. Although computers can help us work out many problems, we still need to discuss some problems face-to-face. 我认为需要。虽然电脑可以帮助我们解决许多问题，但是我们仍然需要面对面讨论一些问题。
Do you think technology will affect people's work in the future? 你认为未来科技会影响人们的工作吗？	Yes, I think so. Modern technology facilitates our life. Work and life are more and more inseparable from modern technology. 是的，我想会影响。现代科技让我们的生活变得便利。工作和生活与现代科技愈加密不可分。
Do you think the advancement of technology is getting faster now than in the past? 你认为当今科技进步比过去要快吗？	Yes. As we all know, new generations of mobile phones can come out within just several months. 是的。众所周知，如今新一代手机可以在几个月内问世。
What do you suggest on people not spending too much time online? 你对人们不该花太多时间上网有什么建议？	It is not good for us to spend too much time online. We can do some healthy activities such as hiking, visiting friends and avoid long hours of computers. 花太多时间上网对我们来说是不好的。我们可以进行一些如远足、拜访朋友等健康活动，避免长时间使用电脑。

"科学技术"高阶问答	
Q我是考官	A我是考生
Do you think the electronic media will take place of the traditional paper media? 你认为电子媒体会取代传统纸媒吗?	No, I don't think so. Although electronic devices are developing very fast, traditional paper media is still very important to our life. When we go to school, we use paper textbooks and exercise books for class and homework. 不，我不这么认为。虽然电子设备发展得非常快，但是传统纸媒对我们的生活仍然很重要。我们在学校上课和写作业，都要用纸质的课本和练习册。
	Yes, I think electronic media will eventually substitute traditional paper media. This is because electronic media offers convenience, allowing people to access information quickly and easily. Additionally, electronic media is more environmentally friendly, as it reduces the need for paper production and waste. 是的，我认为电子媒体最终会取代传统的纸质媒体。这是因为电子媒体提供了便利，使人们能够方便快捷地获取信息。此外，电子媒体更环保，因为它减少了纸张生产和浪费的需要。

科技设备		
phone 手机	smartwatch 智能手表	TV 电视
mobile phone 手机	headset耳机	printer 打印机
smartphone 智能手机	game console 游戏机	scanner 扫描仪
computer电脑	camera相机	keyboard 键盘
tablet computer 平板电脑	digital camera 数码相机	mouse 鼠标
laptop computer 笔记本电脑	iPad 苹果平板电脑	

★必会句型★

1. 介绍"科技进步的好处"

1) As we all know, ... 众所周知，……

2) ... offer us great convenience. ……为我们提供了极大的便利。

3) This is because ... offers convenience. 这是因为……提供了便利。

4) I think we can not only ..., but also ... 我觉得我们不仅可以……，还可以……

5) We can rely on ... to do many things. 我们可以依赖……做很多事情。

6) ... can help us work out many problems. ……可以帮助我们解决许多问题。

7) Technology helps us communicate better. 科技帮助我们更好地沟通。

8) Computer helps us work much more efficiently. 电脑帮助我们更有效地工作。

2. 介绍"科技进步的弊端"

1) Technology is a double-edged sword. 科技是一把双刃剑。

2) Technological advancement has brought many benefits to our lives, but it also has some drawbacks. 科技进步给我们的生活带来了许多好处，但它也有一些缺点。

3) It is not good for our eyes to spend too much time online. 花太多时间上网对我们的眼睛不好。

4) For example, it can lead to less physical activity and more sedentary lifestyles. 例如，它会导致身体活动减少和久坐不动的生活方式。

Day 5　生活常识

 考场模拟

 How many seasons are there in a year in your country?

There are four seasons in my country. They are spring, summer, autumn, and winter.

 思路点拨

Q: **How many seasons are there in a year in your country?** 你们国家一年有几个季节？

There are ＿＿＿＿＿＿＿＿＿＿ in my country. They are ＿＿＿＿＿＿＿＿＿＿.

在我们国家，有＿＿＿＿＿＿＿＿＿＿。它们是＿＿＿＿＿＿＿＿＿＿。

* how many是对数量进行提问，回答用there be句型。How many提问时，后面跟可数名词复数，比如seasons（季节）。此外，考生在作答时不但要给出数量，最好补充说明具体内容，比如They are...。

考点锦囊

"常识"常见问答	
Q我是考官	A我是考生
How many months are there in a year? 一年有几个月?	There are twelve months in a year. They are January, February, March, April, May, June, July, August, September, October, November, and December. 一年有十二个月，分别是一月、二月、三月、四月、五月、六月、七月、八月、九月、十月、十一月和十二月。
How many days are there in a week? 一星期有几天?	There are seven days in a week. They are Monday, Tuesday, Wednesday, Thursday, Friday, Saturday and Sunday. 一星期有七天，分别是星期一、星期二、星期三、星期四、星期五、星期六和星期日。
How many seconds are there in a minute? 一分钟有多少秒?	There are sixty seconds in a minute. 一分钟有六十秒。
How many minutes are there in an hour? 一小时有多少分钟?	There are sixty minutes in an hour. 一小时有六十分钟。
What is five and two? 五加二等于几?	Five and two is seven. 五加二等于七。
What is fifteen minus nine? 十五减九等于几?	Fifteen minus nine is six. 十五减九等于六。

生活常识		
一年四季	一年12个月	每周7天
spring 春天 summer 夏天 autumn/ fall 秋天 winter 冬天	January (Jan.) 1月 February (Feb.) 2月 March (Mar.) 3月 April (Apr.) 4月 May 5月 June (Jun.) 6月 July (Jul.) 7月 August (Aug.) 8月 September (Sept.) 9月 October (Oct.) 10月 November (Nov.) 11月 December (Dec.) 12月	Monday 星期一 Tuesday 星期二 Wednesday 星期三 Thursday 星期四 Friday 星期五 Saturday 星期六 Sunday 星期日

生活常识		
一天	时分秒	星球
a.m. 上午	o'clock（表示整点）……点钟	earth 地球
p.m. 下午	hour 小时	sun 太阳
morning 早上	minute 分钟	moon 月亮
noon 中午	second 秒	star 星星
afternoon 下午	quarter 一刻钟（15分钟）	planet 行星
evening 在晚上		
night 晚上		
midnight 午夜		

★必会句型★

1. 介绍年月日常识

1) There are ... seasons in my country. They are ... 在我国有……个季节，分别是……

2) There are twelve months in a year. They are ... 一年有12个月，分别是……

3) There are seven days in a week. They are ... 一周有7天，分别是……

2. 介绍时分秒常识

1) There are sixty minutes in an hour. 一小时有60分钟。

2) There are sixty seconds in a minute. 一分钟有60秒。

3. 介绍数学加减法常识

1) ... plus... is... ……加……等于……

2) ... minus ... is ... ……减……等于……

Weekend 三 每周一练

I. 选一选，选出最合适的答语。

( ) 1. Q: When do you usually watch TV?

A) We celebrate New Year in our country.

B) My pet cat's name is Poppy.

C) I usually watch TV on weekends.

(　) 2.　Q: How often do you go to the zoo?

　　　　A) About twice a year.

　　　　B) Action films are more exciting.

　　　　C) There are twelve months in a year.

(　) 3.　Q: How many seconds are there in a minute?

　　　　A) There are sixty seconds in a minute.

　　　　B) I haven't had a pet ever.

　　　　C) There are many festivals in China.

(　) 4.　Q: What animals do you like?

　　　　A) My pet is quiet.

　　　　B) It has golden hair.

　　　　C) I like dogs.

(　) 5.　Q: What is four plus three?

　　　　A) It is seven.

　　　　B) The bird is cute.

　　　　C) I like cartoons best.

(　) 6.　Q: What kind of movies do you like?

　　　　A) I have a pet dog.

　　　　B) There are seven days in a week.

　　　　C) I prefer science fiction movies.

Ⅱ. 读一读，圈出正确的单词。

1. I like playing *with / about* my pet.

2. I can *spend / cost* more time with my family during the festival.

3. There *is / are* four seasons in a year.

4. My pet *has / is* big eyes.

5. Five *plus / minus* one is six.

6. I like comedies *because / so* they are funny.

7. My favourite thing is *listen / listening* to music on the Internet.

8. The Dragon Boat Festival is quite popular *on / in* my country.

9. How many seconds are *there / here* in a minute?

10. Technology *will / would* affect people's work in the future.

III. 将左右两列的相应内容连线，构成完整的一句话。

1. I like	A. are very popular nowadays.
2. The Spring Festival	B. four seasons in a year.
3. Smartphones	C. is one of the most important festivals.
4. There are	D. pandas very much.
5. I usually go	E. faithful to their masters.
6. Dogs are	F. with my pet cat.
7. We celebrate	G. New Year in my country.
8. I like playing	H. to the cinema once a month.

IV. 判断下面句子正误，如有错，请圈出并将正确形式写在下面的横线上。

1. What are five plus two?

_____

2. Mid-Autumn festival is special time in my country.

_____

3. The technological progress is getting fast now than before.

_____

4. How often do you go to the cinema?

_____

5. How many pets do you had?

_____

6. Have your brother got a new smart phone?

_____

7. What TV programme are you like best?

_____

8. Ten minus nine is one.

_____

V. 连词成句。

1. Sam's / short / is / hair / very /.

   _____

2. All / have / my / got / friends / laptops /.

   _____

3. The end / film / is / of / too / this / sad /.

   _____

4. Teenagers / other / don't / each / very / email / often /.

   _____

5. What / excited / makes / most / you /?

   _____

6. receives / Who / good / on / wishes / days / special /?

   _____

7. a / She / use / couldn't / computer / three / when / was / she /.

   _____

8. phone / My / can / do / things / lots of /.

   _____

VI. 模拟演练。

>>**Activity 1 Programmes**

Examiner: Now, in this part of the test you are going to talk together. Here are some pictures that show **different TV programmes**. Do you like these different types of TV programmes? Say why or why not. I'll say that again. Do you like these different types of TV programmes? Say why or why not. All right? Now, talk together.

Candidate B: Do you like watching the news on TV?

Candidate A: 1. _____

Examiner: Do you think watching cartoons is fun?

Candidate A/B: 2. _____

Examiner: Do you think watching football matches is exciting?

Candidate A/B: 3. _____

Examiner: Which of these TV programmes do you like best?

Candidate A/B: 4. _____

>>Activity 2 Festivals

Examiner: Now, in this part of the test you are going to talk together. Here are some pictures that show **different festivals**. Do you like these different festivals? Say why or why not. I'll say that again. Do you like these different festivals? Say why or why not. All right? Now, talk together.

Candidate B: Do you like the Spring Festival?

Candidate A: 5. _____

Examiner: Do you think the Dragon Boat Festival is fun?

Candidate A/B: 6. _____

Examiner: Do you think New Year is a special time?

Candidate A/B: 7. _____

Examiner: Which of these festivals do you like best?

Candidate A/B: 8. _____

Part 2 方位地点

考试模块	时间	话题	我是考官	我是考生	
			第7周目标		
Part 2 方位地点	Day 1	房屋住宿	Which is your favourite room in your house?	My favourite room is... I can...	☐
	Day 2	购物场所	Do you like going shopping online?	Yes, I do. It's... No, I don't. It's...	☐
	Day 3	用餐场所	How often do you and your family go to a restaurant?	My family and I go there...	☐
	Day 4	城市去处	Where do you like to go in the city?	I like... There are...	☐
	Day 5	地方建筑	Are there any historical buildings around your house?	Yes, there're... No, there're not...	☐
	Weekend	每周一练	每周基础知识练习		☐

Day 1 房屋住宿

 考场模拟

 Which is your favourite room in your house?

My favourite room is the playhouse. I can play with my friends in it.

思路点拨

Q: **Which is your favourite room in your house?** 你最喜欢家里哪个房间？

My favourite room is _____. I can _____.

我最喜欢的房间是_____。我可以_____。

*考生在回答时不但要表明观点，还要尽量扩展答案，尽可能给出原因和例子，如I can play with my friends in it.（我可以和我的朋友在里面玩。）

考点锦囊

"房屋住宿" 常见问答	
Q我是考官	A我是考生
How many rooms are there in your house? 你家里有几个房间？	There are four rooms in my house. They're two bedrooms, one living room and one study room. 我家里有四个房间，分别是两间卧室、一间客厅和一间书房。
Do you like your bedroom? 你喜欢你的卧室吗？	Yes, I like it very much because there are lots of toys in my bedroom. 是的，我非常喜欢它，因为我的卧室里有很多玩具。
Where do you do your homework at home? 你在家时在哪里写作业？	I usually do my homework in the study room. It's so quiet that I can focus on my homework. 我通常在书房做作业。书房很安静，我可以专心做作业。

"房屋住宿" 高阶问答	
Q我是考官	A我是考生
Please tell me something about your house. 请告诉我一些关于你的房子的事情。	My house is a cozy place to live. It has a living room, two bedrooms, and a kitchen. I love spending time with my family in our house. 我家房子住起来很舒适。它有一个客厅、两间卧室和一个厨房。我喜欢和家人待在家里。
	My house is a cozy two-storey building. It has a red roof and white walls. The living room is my favourite place, as it has a comfortable sofa, a big TV, and a bookshelf filled with my favourite books. 我家的房子是一栋舒适的两层楼房。它有红色的屋顶和白色的墙壁。客厅是我最喜欢的地方，因为那儿有一个舒适的沙发、一个大电视，还有一个书架，里面摆满了我最喜欢的书。
	My house is located on the 9th floor of a building in the city centre. It is a comfortable place where my family and I live together. 我家位于市中心一栋大楼的9楼。这是一个舒适的地方，我和我的家人住在一起。

描述房屋常用词		
房间	室内物品	家电
living room 客厅	chair 椅子	air conditioning 空调系统
sitting room 起居室	desk 书桌	battery 电池
study room 书房	table 桌子	frying pan 煎锅
bathroom 浴室	wardrobe 衣柜	television(TV) 电视
shower 淋浴间	cupboard 橱柜	hairdryer 吹风机
kitchen 厨房	cabinet 贮藏柜	lamp 灯
dining room 餐厅	bookshelf 书架	washing machine 洗衣机
bedroom 卧室	drawer 抽屉	video recorder 录像机
playhouse 儿童游戏房	bed 床	
basement 地下室	armchair 扶手椅	
washroom 洗手间	sofa 沙发	
balcony 阳台		

★ **必会句型** ★

1. **介绍家的位置**

   1) My house is located on the ... floor of a building in the city centre. 我家位于市中心一栋大楼的……楼。

   2) My home is on the 2nd floor of an apartment building. 我家在一栋公寓楼的二楼。

   3) My house is a cozy two-storey building. 我家是一栋舒适的两层楼房。

2. **介绍家里几个房间**

   1) There are ... rooms in my house. 我家里有……个房间。

   2) It has a living room, ...bedrooms, and a kitchen. 它有一间客厅、……间卧室和一间厨房。

3. **介绍喜欢的房间**

   1) My favourite room is ... I can ... 我最喜欢的房间是……。我可以……

   2) I like ... very much because ... 我非常喜欢……，因为……

   3) I usually do my homework in ... 我通常在……写作业。

   4) It's so quiet that I can focus on my homework. 这里很安静，我可以专心写作业。

5) The living room is my favourite place, as it has a comfortable sofa... and a bookshelf filled with my favourite books. 客厅是我最喜欢的地方，因为那儿有一个舒适的沙发……，还有一个书架，里面摆满了我最喜欢的书。

6) It has a red roof and white walls. 它有红色的屋顶和白色的墙壁。

4. 介绍家庭氛围

1) My house is a cozy place to live. 我的家是一个温馨舒适的居所。

2) I love spending time with my family in our house. 我喜欢和家人待在家里。

3) It is a comfortable place where my family and I live together. 这是一个舒适的地方，我和家人住在一起。

Day 2　购物场所

 考场模拟

 Do you like going shopping online?

Yes, I like shopping online. It's very convenient.

 思路点拨

Q: **Do you like going shopping online?** 你喜欢在网上购物吗？

Yes, I _____ . It's _____ .

是的，我_____。它是_____。

/ No, I don't_____ . It's _____ .

不，我不_____。它是_____。

*在回答do引导的一般疑问句Do...? 时，除了要用到Yes/ No，还要在yes或no的基础上进一步说明情况。

考点锦囊

"购物场所" 常见问答	
Q我是考官	A我是考生
Do you like going shopping at the supermarket? 你喜欢去超市购物吗?	Yes, I can buy some snacks and fresh fruits at the supermarket. 是的, 我可以在超市买到一些零食和新鲜水果。
Do you think markets are cheap? 你认为集市便宜吗?	Sure. There's always a sale going on. 当然, 集市总有打折。
	Yes, markets can be cheap when there are sales or discounts available. 是的, 当有促销或折扣时, 市场可能很便宜。
	It depends, markets can be cheap or expensive. 这要看情况, 市场可能便宜, 也可能贵。
Do you think shopping online is interesting? 你认为网上购物有趣吗?	I think so. I can buy something fashionable on the Internet. 我想是的。我可以在网上买到一些时髦的东西。
	No, I don't think shopping online is interesting because I prefer to see and touch products in person before making a purchase. 不, 我不认为网上购物有趣, 因为我更喜欢在购买之前亲自看到和触摸商品。

"购物场所" 高阶问答	
Q我是考官	A我是考生
Do you prefer to go shopping on your own or with someone else? Why? 你更喜欢一个人去购物还是和别人一起去? 为什么?	I like to go shopping with my mum because she helps me choose nice things and it's fun to spend time together. 我喜欢和妈妈一起去购物, 因为她会帮我挑选好东西, 而且和妈妈在一起很有趣。
	I prefer going shopping with my friends. I can get opinions and suggestions from my shopping companion. 我更喜欢和朋友去购物。我可以从我的购物伙伴那里得到意见和建议。
What's the best way to buy things cheaply? Why? 买到便宜东西的最好方法是什么? 为什么?	I think the best way is to go to the discount shops. They regularly sell goods at a low price. It's a good way to save money. 我认为最好的方法是去折扣店。他们经常以低价出售商品。那是省钱的好方法。
	The best way to buy things cheaply is to look for discounts or sales. This helps to save money and get the best deal possible. 买便宜东西的最好方法是寻找折扣或促销活动。这有助于省钱, 并达成最划算的交易。

购物场所		
shopping mall 购物中心	shop 商店	supermarket 超市
shopping centre 购物中心	retail store 零售店	bookstore 书店
department store 百货商场	store 商店	bookshop 书店
clothing store 服装店	market 市场	flower shop 花店
superstore 超级商场	mall 购物商场	chemist 药店
shoe store 鞋店	convenience store 便利店	toy store 玩具店
shopping online 网上购物	grocer 食品杂货店	

促销活动		
sale 促销	special offer 特别优惠	discount price 折扣价格
discount 折扣	discount offer 打折优惠	at a discount 打折扣
giveaway 赠品	flash sale 限时促销	10% off 九折
coupon 优惠券	member discount 会员折扣	15% discount 八五折
loyalty card 积分卡	clearance sale 清仓特卖	full price 全价

★ 必会句型 ★

1. 介绍购物场所

1) I can buy ... at the supermarket. 我可以在超市买到……

2) I can buy ... on the Internet. 我可以在网上买到……

2. 介绍购物性价比

1) The best way to buy things cheaply is to .... 买便宜东西的最好方法是……

2) I think the best way is to go to ... 我认为最好的方法是去……

3) It's a good way to save money. 那是省钱的好方法。

4) ... regularly sell goods at a low price. ……经常以低价出售商品。

5) There's always a sale there. 那里总有打折。

6) ... can be cheap when there are sales or discounts available. 当有促销或折扣时，……可能很便宜。

7) This helps to save money and .... 这有助于省钱，并……

3. 介绍购物习惯

1) I prefer going shopping with ... 我更喜欢和……去购物。

2) She helps me choose nice things. 她帮我挑选好东西。

3) I don't think ... is interesting. 我不认为……有趣。

4) I can get opinions from ... 我可以从……那里得到意见。

Day 3　用餐场所

 考场模拟

How often do you and your family go to a restaurant?

My family and I go there almost once a week.

 思路点拨

Q: **How often do you and your family go to a restaurant?** 你和家人多久去一次餐馆?

My family and I go there ＿＿＿＿＿＿＿＿＿＿＿＿.

我和我的家人＿＿＿＿＿＿＿＿＿＿去那里。

*how often意为"多久一次",对频率提问。考试中常问到的问题包括"多久去一次哪里""多久做一次什么"等,答语要包括做某件事情的频率,如once a week。

 考点锦囊

"用餐场所"常见问答	
Q我是考官	A我是考生
Do you often go to fast food restaurants? 你经常去快餐店吗?	Yes, I go there quite often. I like going with my friends. We can eat and talk there. 是的,我经常去那里。我喜欢和朋友们一起去。我们可以在那里吃饭、聊天。
Where do you usually have lunch? 你通常在哪里吃午饭?	I usually have lunch at school. 我通常在学校吃午饭。
Where do you usually have dinner? 你通常在哪里吃晚饭?	I usually have dinner at home. 我通常在家里吃晚饭。

续表

"用餐场所" 常见问答	
Q我是考官	A我是考生
Do you like eating at fast food restaurants? 你喜欢在快餐店吃饭吗?	No, I don't like eating at fast food restaurants because the food is not healthy. 不,我不喜欢在快餐店吃饭,因为那里的食物不健康。
	Yes, I like eating at fast food restaurants because they serve delicious food and it's quick and convenient. 是的,我喜欢在快餐店吃饭,因为他们提供美味的食物,而且快捷方便。
Do you like eating at school? 你喜欢在学校吃饭吗?	No. I don't like eating at school because the food is not very tasty. 不。我不喜欢在学校吃饭,因为食物不是很好吃。
Do you like having a picnic in the park? 你喜欢在公园里野餐吗?	Yes, I like having a picnic in the park with my family. It's relaxing. 我喜欢和家人在公园野餐,这很放松。

"用餐场所" 高阶问答	
Q我是考官	A我是考生
Do you think having a picnic in the park is cheap? 你认为在公园里野餐便宜吗?	Yes, I agree. I can bring my own food and enjoy the outdoor surroundings without spending much money. 是的,我同意。我可以自己带食物,不用花很多钱就能享受户外环境。
Do you think fast food restaurants are convenient? 你认为快餐店方便吗?	Yes, they are very convenient. We don't need to wait for the food for too long. And we can either eat in the restaurant or take the food out. 是的,快餐店很方便。我们不需要等太久。我们可以在店里吃,也可以把食物打包。
Which is your favourite restaurant? Why? 你最喜欢的餐馆是哪个? 为什么?	I like the restaurant near my home best because the food there is tasty and it's only about five minutes' walk from my home. 我最喜欢家附近的那家餐馆,因为那里的食物很好吃,而且从我家走到那里只有五分钟的路程。

用餐场所	
Chinese restaurant 中餐厅	snack bar 小吃店
buffet restaurant 自助餐厅	food truck 食品车
take-out restaurant 外卖店	Italian restaurant 意大利餐厅
fast food restaurant 快餐店	eat at school 在学校吃饭
go to a restaurant 去餐厅	go to a cafeteria 去自助餐厅
eat at home 在家吃饭	have a picnic in the park 在公园野餐

★ *必会句型* ★

1. 介绍用餐地点

1) I usually have lunch at ... 我通常在……吃午饭。

2) I usually have dinner at ... 我通常在……吃晚饭。

3) I go ... quite often. 我经常去……

4) I like ... with my friends. 我喜欢和朋友们一起……

5) I like having a picnic in ... with ... It's relaxing. 我喜欢和……在……野餐，这很放松。

6) We can either eat in ... or ... 我们可以在……吃，也可以在……吃。

7) We can eat and talk ... 我们可以在……吃饭、聊天。

8) My family and I go to a restaurant twice a week. 我和家人每周去两次餐馆。

2. 介绍喜欢的餐馆

1) I like ... best because the food there is ... 我最喜欢……，因为那里的食物……

2) I don't like eating at ... because the food is ... 我不喜欢在……吃饭，因为食物……

3) I like the restaurant near my home best because... 我最喜欢家附近的那家餐馆，因为……

4) I like having a picnic in the park with my family. It's relaxing. 我喜欢和家人在公园野餐，这很放松。

5) The lunch at school is ... 学校午餐……

3. 介绍对餐馆的看法

1) It's not healthy to eat at ... 在……吃东西不健康。

2) We don't need to wait for the food for too long. 我们等上菜不需要太久。

3) We can either eat in the restaurant or take the food out. 我们可以在店里吃，也可以把食物打包。

4) It's only about ... minutes' walk from my home. 从我家走到那里大概只有……分钟的路程。

Day 4　城市去处

 考场模拟

Where do you like to go in the city?

I like to go to the library. There are all kinds of books in the library.

 思路点拨

Q:　**Where do you like to go in the city? 你喜欢去城市里的什么地方？**

I like ＿＿＿＿＿＿＿＿＿＿＿＿. There are ＿＿＿＿＿＿＿＿＿＿＿＿.

我喜欢＿＿＿＿＿＿＿＿＿＿＿。有＿＿＿＿＿＿＿＿＿＿＿。

*在回答地点类问题时，考生不但要给出明确地点，最好再解释一下原因。

 考点锦囊

"城市去处" 常见问答	
Q我是考官	A我是考生
Is there a sports centre near your home? 你家附近有体育中心吗？	Yes, there is a sports centre near my home. I go there almost every weekend. 是的，我家附近有一个体育中心。我几乎每个周末都去那里。
Do you often go to the amusement park? 你经常去游乐场吗？	Not very often. The amusement park is far from my house and I don't have much free time. 不经常。游乐园离我家很远，我没有太多的空闲时间。
	Yes, I often go to the amusement park because I love the fun rides and games there. 是的，我经常去游乐园，因为我喜欢那里的游乐设施和游戏。
Do you like visiting the museum? 你喜欢参观博物馆吗？	Yes, I like visiting the museum because I can learn something new from there. 是的，我喜欢参观博物馆，因为我可以从那里学到新的东西。

续表

"城市去处"常见问答	
Q我是考官	A我是考生
How often do you go to a park? 你多久去一次公园？	I go to a park **almost every evening**. 我几乎每晚都去公园。

"城市去处"高阶问答	
Q我是考官	A我是考生
Do you think going to Universal Studio is fun? 你觉得去环球影城好玩吗？	**Yes**, I like Transformers and Harry Potter and the Escape from Gringotts the most. 好玩，我最喜欢变形金刚和哈利·波特与古灵阁大逃亡。
Do you think cinemas are exciting? 你认为电影院令人兴奋吗？	**No**, I prefer to watch films at home. 不，我更喜欢在家看电影。
Do you think parks are important? 你认为公园重要吗？	**Yes**, they are really important. There are many places to take a rest and have fun with friends or family in the park. 是的，公园真的很重要。公园里有很多可供朋友或家人一起休息和玩耍的地方。
Where do you think is the best place in this city? Why? 你认为这个城市最好的地方是哪里？为什么？	Well, I think the **gallery** is the best place **because** the gallery is filled with beautiful works of art. 嗯，我认为美术馆是最好的去处，因为美术馆里摆满了漂亮的艺术作品。
Do you prefer going back to the same places in your city or going to lots of different places? Why? 在你所在的城市，你更喜欢去同一个地方还是去不同的地方？为什么？	I prefer to **go to lots of different places**. I like discovering new things. 我更喜欢去很多不同的地方。我喜欢发现新事物。

城市去处		
cinema 电影院	sports centre 体育中心	bookstore 书店
museum 博物馆	cafe 咖啡馆	park 公园
library 图书馆	movie theatre 电影院	square 广场
post office 邮局	gallery 展览馆	bank 银行
amusement park 游乐场	art gallery 美术馆	

★必会句型★

1. 介绍喜欢去的场所

1) I prefer to ... 我更喜欢……

2) I prefer to go to lots of different places. 我更喜欢去很多不同的地方。

3) I like visiting ... because I can learn ... from there. 我喜欢参观……，因为我可以从那里学到……

4) I like discovering new things. 我喜欢发现新事物。

2. 介绍自己家附近的场所

1) There is a(n) ... near my home. 我家附近有一个……

2) I go there almost every ... 我几乎每……都去那里。

3) The... is far from my house. ……离我家很远。

3. 介绍城市好去处

1) I think ... is the best place because ... 我认为……是最好的去处，因为……

2) I often go to ... because I love ... there. 我经常去……，因为我喜欢那里的……

3) There are many places to take a rest and have fun. ……有很多可供休息和玩耍的地方。

 Day 5 地方建筑

 考场模拟

Are there any historical buildings around your house?

Yes, there're some famous historical buildings around my house such as the National Museum. These buildings are built many years ago. Thousands of people come to visit each year.

 思路点拨

Q: **Are there any historical buildings around your house?** 你家周围有什么历史建筑吗？

Yes, there're ＿＿＿＿＿＿＿＿＿＿＿＿.

是的，有＿＿＿＿＿＿＿＿＿＿＿＿＿。

/ No, there're not ＿＿＿＿＿＿＿＿＿＿＿＿＿.

/不，没有＿＿＿＿＿＿＿＿＿＿＿＿＿。

*回答there be一般疑问句时，首先要回答Yes, there're... 或者No, there're not...，然后进一步阐述。

 考点锦囊

"地方建筑" 常见问答	
Q我是考官	A我是考生
Which of these buildings: skyscrapers, shopping malls, country cottage, etc. do you prefer to go? 摩天大楼、购物中心、乡村小屋等建筑，你更想要去哪里？	I prefer to go to skyscrapers because I can overlook the city view from the top of the skyscraper. 我更喜欢去摩天大楼，因为我可以从摩天大楼的最高处俯瞰城市的景色。
	I prefer to go to country cottages because they allow me to relax and enjoy nature. 我更喜欢去乡村小屋，因为它们让我放松和享受自然。
	I prefer to go to shopping malls because there are a wide variety of stores and entertainment options. 我更喜欢去购物中心，因为这里有各种各样的商店和娱乐选择。
Which do you think will be more fun, going to the countryside or to the mountains? 你觉得去乡下和去山里，哪个更有趣？	I think going to the countryside is more fun. The air in the countryside is very fresh. And I can play with my friends there. 我觉得去乡下更有趣。乡下的空气很新鲜。而且我还可以和朋友一起玩。
	I think going to the mountains will be more fun because I can enjoy the beautiful scenery and have exciting outdoor activities such as hiking and skiing. 我认为去山上会更有趣，因为我可以欣赏美丽的风景，并进行令人兴奋的户外活动，如远足和滑雪。
Please tell me something about one place of interest in your hometown or country. 请告诉我你家乡或国家的一处名胜。	The Palace Museum is one of the most famous places of interest in China. It was the Chinese imperial palace from the Mid-Ming Dynasty to the end of the Qing Dynasty. Each year lots of tourists come to visit it. 故宫博物院是中国最著名的名胜之一。它曾是明朝中期至清朝末期的中国皇宫。每年都有很多游客来参观。

名胜古迹	
The Forbidden City/ The Palace Museum 故宫	The West Lake 西湖
The Summer Palace 颐和园	Three Gorges 长江三峡
The Great Wall 长城	Suzhou Gardens 苏州园林

名胜古迹	
Tian'anmen Square 天安门广场	The Temple of Heaven 天坛
Longmen Grottoes 龙门石窟	Big Wild Goose Pagoda 大雁塔
Dujiang Dam 都江堰	Yueyang Tower 岳阳楼
Qin Terra-Cotta Warriors and Horses Figurines 秦始皇兵马俑	Tower of Yellow Crane 黄鹤楼

城市建筑		
skyscraper 摩天大楼	arch 拱门	tower bridge 塔桥
tower 塔楼	cathedral 大教堂	stone arch 石拱门
bridge 桥梁	statue 雕塑	church 教堂
monument 纪念碑		

★ 必会句型 ★

1. 介绍喜欢去的地方建筑

1) I prefer... because ... 我更喜欢……，因为……

2) I think going to ... is more fun. 我觉得去……更有趣。

2. 介绍喜欢去的原因

1) The air ... is very fresh. ……的空气很新鲜。

2) You can enjoy the beautiful scenery. 你可以欣赏美丽的风景。

3) They offer a cozy and peaceful atmosphere, allowing me to relax and enjoy nature. 它们提供了一个舒适和宁静的氛围，让我放松和享受自然。

4) There are a wide variety of ... and entertainment options. 这里有各种各样的……和娱乐选择。

5) You can have exciting outdoor activities such as ... 你可以有令人兴奋的户外活动，如……

6) I can overlook the city view from the top of ... 我可以从……的最高处俯瞰城市的景色。

3. 介绍名胜古迹

1) There're some famous historical buildings around my house such as ... 我家周围有一些著名的历史建筑，比如……

2) The building is built ... years ago. 这栋楼是……年前建的。

3) Thousands of people come to visit ... each year. 每年都有成千上万的人来参观……

4) ... is one of the most famous places of interest in China. ······是中国最著名的名胜之一。

Weekend 三 每周一练

I. 选一选，选出最合适的答语。

( ) 1. Q: Where do you usually buy your clothes?

A) I usually go shopping online.

B) My family and I go there almost every week.

C) I usually do my homework in the study room.

( ) 2. Q: How many rooms are there in your house?

A) Yes, I like it very much.

B) There are three rooms in my house.

C) There is always a sale in markets.

( ) 3. Q: Where do you like going in the city?

A) Thousands of people visit it.

B) The air in the park is fresh.

C) I like going to the library.

( ) 4. Q: How often do you go on holiday?

A) Maybe once or twice a year.

B) I like painting and dancing.

C) It's ten minutes' walk.

( ) 5. Q: Where do you usually have lunch?

A) I usually have lunch at school.

B) I watch TV in the living room.

C) I go to school at 7 o'clock.

( ) 6. Q: How much are those books you bought?

A) There are sixty minutes.

B) They cost 150 yuan.

C) I have little homework to do.

II. 读一读，圈出正确的单词。

1. Is there a sports centre *near / from* your house?

2. Do you *have / has* any plan for this weekend?

3. How many *rooms / room* are there in your house?

4. I *don't / doesn't* like in-store shopping.

5. How often do you *went / go* to a park?

6. I can buy all the *things / thing* I like.

7. Where do you usually buy *your / you* clothes?

8. My dad *took / take* a lot of photos yesterday.

9. Do all of your family have free *time / times* every weekend?

10. The pants *cost / took* me 200 yuan.

III. 将左右两列的相应内容连线，构成完整的一句话。

1. The buildings   A. books in the study room.

2. I usually have   B. goods at a low price.

3. They regularly sell   C. are built many years ago.

4. I can read   D. lunch at school.

5. She always buys her clothes   E. leave the house today.

6. We all have free   F. really happy.

7. I'm not going to   G. time every weekend.

8. Susan looks   H. at a shopping mall.

IV. 判断下面句子正误，如有错，请圈出并将正确形式写在下面的横线上。

1. There are five rooms in my house.

2. It is good way to save money.

3. Does you often go to the library?

4. There are all kind of things in the mall. ☐

_____

5. Are you sleeping when I phoned you? ☐

_____

6. Does Marco wants to come with us? ☐

_____

7. It was so windy that my hat came off. ☐

_____

8. People like to going to this place next to the sea. ☐

_____

V. 连词成句。

1. Fast / healthy / food / is / never /.

_____

2. We / can / to / walk / it / the / park / is / because / not far /.

_____

3. open / The / on / museum / is / Sundays /.

_____

4. countryside / is / The air / in / the / very / fresh /.

_____

5. don't / We / to / need / wait / too / for / long /.

_____

6. What / buy / is / to / things / the / way / cheaply / best /?

_____

7. to / I / lots / prefer / of / to / different / go / places /.

_____

8. always / There / a / is / going / sale / on /.

_____

VI. 模拟演练。

>>Activity 1 Places to eat

Examiner: Now, in this part of the test you are going to talk together. Here are some pictures that show **different places to eat**. Do you like these different places to eat? Say why or why not. I'll say that again. Do you like these different places to eat? Say why or why not. All right? Now, talk together.

Candidate B: Do you like eating at school?

Candidate A: 1. _____

Examiner: Do you think fast food is healthy?

Candidate A/B: 2. _____

Examiner: Do you think eating at home is boring?

Candidate A/B: 3. _____

Examiner: Which of these places do you prefer to have a meal?

Candidate A/B: 4. _____

>>Activity 2 Places in city

Examiner: Now, in this part of the test you are going to talk together. Here are some pictures that show **different places in city**. Do you like these different places in city? Say why or why not. I'll say that again. Do you like these different places in city? Say why or why not. All right? Now, talk together.

Candidate B: Do you like playing in the sports centre?

Candidate A: 5. _____

Examiner: Do you think going to the museum is fun?

Candidate A/B: 6. _____

Examiner: Do you think parks are enjoyable?

Candidate A/B: 7. _____

Examiner: Which of these places in city do you like best?

Candidate A/B: 8. _____

8

考试全流程模拟练习

第8周目标			
考试模块	时间	话题	
考试全流程 模拟练习	Day 1 ~ Day 5 Weekend	Part 1-1 姓名、问候、年龄及来自哪里	☐
		Part 1-2 语言、交通	☐
		Part 2 动物宠物	☐

Part 1-1   姓名、问候、年龄及来自哪里

Part 1 (3~4 minutes)

Phase 1

Examiner:	Good morning. Can I have your mark sheets, please? I'm Jenny and this is Kate. What's your name, please?
Candidate A/B:	1. _____
Examiner:	How is it going?
Candidate A/B:	2. _____
Examiner:	Where are you from?
Candidate A/B:	3. _____
Examiner:	How old are you?
Candidate A/B:	4. _____

Part 1-2   语言、交通

Phase 2

Examiner:	Now, let's talk about **language**.

A, which foreign language are you studying at your school?

Candidate A:	5. _____
Examiner:	How long have you studied English?
Candidate A:	6. _____
Examiner:	B, do you read English every day?
Candidate B:	7. _____
Examiner:	Is English hard or easy for you?
Candidate B:	8. _____
Examiner:	Now A, please tell me something about your favourite language.
Candidate A:	9. _____

Examiner:	Now, let's talk about **traffic**.
	B, how do you get to school every day?
Candidate B:	10. _____
Examiner:	Do you like travelling by airplane?
Candidate B:	11. _____
Examiner:	A, how did you get here this morning?
Candidate A:	12. _____
Examiner:	How do you like to travel if you are going on a long journey?
Candidate A:	13. _____
Examiner:	Now B, please tell me something about your favourite public traffic.
Candidate B:	14. _____

Part 2 动物宠物

Part 2 (5~6 minutes)

Do you like these different animals? Say why or why not.

Phase 1

Examiner: Now, in this part of the test you are going to talk together.

(Place Part 2 booklet, open at Task 2, in front of candidates.)

Here are some pictures that show **different animals**.

Do you like these animals? Say why or why not.

I'll say that again.

Do you like these animals? Say why or why not.

All right? Now, talk together.

【考生对话】

Candidate A: _____

Candidate B: _____

Candidate A: _____

Candidate B: _____

Candidate A: _____

Candidate B: _____

Allow a minimum of 1 minute (maximum of 2 minutes)

before moving on to the following questions

【考官问答】

Examiner: B, do you think hamsters are cute?

Candidate B: 1. _____

Examiner:	A, do you think puppies are annoying?
Candidate A:	2. _____
Examiner:	B, do you think keeping a parrot is fun?
Candidate B:	3. _____
Examiner:	A, do you think kittens are the best pet to keep?
Candidate A:	4. _____
Examiner:	So, A/ B, which of these animals do you like best?
Candidate A/B:	5. _____
	Thank you.

Phase 2

Examiner:	Now, do you prefer to go to the zoo or keep a pet at home? Why?
Candidate A/B:	6. _____
Examiner:	Which is more popular, large animals or small animals?
Candidate A/B:	7. _____
Examiner:	Thank you. That is the end of the test.

参考答案

Week 2 每周一练

I 1. A 　2. C 　3. B 　4. C 　5. B 　6. B

II 1. is 　2. near 　3. years 　4. see 　5. an 　6. were 　7. do 　8. any

9. doing 　10. your

III 1. B 　2. A 　3. D 　4. C 　5. F 　6. E 　7. H 　8. G

IV 1. × sisters改为sister 　2. × are改为do 或 删除come 　3. √

4. × What改为How 　5. × is改为are 　6. × are改为is

7. × on改为in 　8. × is改为are

V 1. What is your name? 你叫什么名字？

2. My given name is Yang. 我的名字是阳。

3. Are you from China? 你来自中国吗？

4. They live in this city. 他们住在这个城市。

5. When were you born? 你是什么时候出生的？

6. Where is your birthplace? 你的出生地是哪里？

7. I am pretty good. 我很好。

8. How do you spell it? 你怎么拼写它？

VI 1. I'm fine. 我很好。

2. My name is Li Yang. 我的名字叫李阳。

3. I was born on Mar. 23th, 2012. 我出生于2012年3月23日。

4. I come from Guangzhou. 我来自广州。

5. Sure, my name is Xu Nan. 当然可以，我叫许楠。

6. I'm 12 years old. 我今年12岁。

7. Yes, I'm from Beijing. 是的，我来自北京。

8. Yes, I live with my parents. 是的，我和父母住在一起。

Week 3 每周一练

I 1. C 　2. B 　3. A 　4. C 　5. A 　6. B

II 1. in   2. have   3. lot   4. by   5. in   6. spoken   7. minutes   8. wear

9. at   10. drink

III 1. C   2. D   3. B   4. A   5. F   6. E   7. H   8. G

IV 1. × speaks改为speak   2. × does改为do   3. × minute改为minutes

4. √   5. × wants改为want   6. × 删除a

7. × costs改为cost   8. √

V 1. Which class are you in? 你在哪个班级？

2. My school / house is close to my house / school. 我的学校离我家很近/我家离我的学校很近。

3. I am studying English at my school. 我在学校学英语。

4. English is a bit difficult for me. 英语对我来说有点难。

5. I usually wear a dress. 我通常穿裙子。

6. Her favourite food is the hamburger. 她最喜欢的食物是汉堡包。

7. It is raining outside. 外面正在下雨。

8. I often have porridge for breakfast. 我早餐经常喝粥。

VI 1. It's cloudy today. A little bit cold. 今天多云，有点儿冷。

2. Yes, it will be warm and sunny tomorrow. 是的，明天会暖和的，阳光明媚。/

No, it won't be warm. The forcast says it's going to rain. 不，不会暖和。天气预报说有雨。

3. I usually play basketball with my friends outdoors. 我通常和朋友在户外打篮球。

4. My favourite season is summer. It's so hot and sunny that I can go swimming and enjoy ice cream every day. 我最喜欢的季节是夏天。夏天天气很热，阳光明媚，我每天都可以去游泳，享用冰激凌。

5. I am studying at the Beijing NO.1 Experimental Primary School. 我在北京第一实验小学学习。

6. I am in Grade Five. 我在五年级。

7. I usually go to school at 8 o'clock in the morning. 我通常在早上八点去学校。

8. My favourite subject is PE. I love doing sports and playing games with my classmates. 我最喜欢的科目是体育。我喜欢和同学一起做运动和玩游戏。

Week 4 每周一练

I   1. C   2. B   3. B   4. C   5. A   6. C

II   1. meet   2. going   3. ourselves   4. plane   5. did

       6. a   7. bus   8. on   9. do   10. am

III   1. D   2. C   3. B   4. A   5. G   6. H   7. E   8. F

IV   1. × a改为the   2. × learns改为learn   3. × had后面加a

       4. √   5. √   6. × kinds改为kind

       7. × years改为year   8. × are改为is

V   1. I like shopping online. 我喜欢在网上购物。

       2. Have you ever been to a concert? 你去过音乐会吗?

       3. I usually go to school on foot. 我通常步行去上学。

       4. How much is your T-shirt? 你的T恤多少钱?

       5. Can you play a musical instrument? 你会演奏乐器吗?

       6. How do you usually go travelling? 你通常怎么去旅行?

       7. I chat with my friends online. 我和朋友在网上聊天。

       8. Do you have any plans for this Sunday? 这周日你有什么计划吗?

VI   1. Yes, we have summer holidays in August. 是的, 我们在八月放暑假。

       2. I want to go abroad with my parents. 我想和父母一起出国。

       3. Yes, I have been to Australia. 是的, 我去过澳大利亚。

       4. I had a wonderful trip last holiday. I went to Australia with my parents. We visited Sydney Opera and saw koalas. 上个假期我有一次愉快的旅行。我和父母一起去了澳大利亚。我们参观了悉尼歌剧院, 还看到了考拉。

       5. Yes, I like pop music very much. 是的, 我非常喜欢流行音乐。

       6. I listen to music once a week. 我每周听一次音乐。

       7. I think songs that can easily be learnt are popular. 我认为容易学的歌曲会受欢迎。

       8. My favourite singer is Wang. She is good at singing. She is very popular on TikTok. 我最喜欢的歌手是王。她擅长唱歌。她在抖音上很受欢迎。

Week 5 每周一练

I   1. B   2. A   3. C   4. C   5. C   6. A

II 1. a   2. chat   3. is   4. swimming   5. wears   6. for

7. engineer   8. weekend   9. because   10. once

III 1. D   2. A   3. B   4. C   5. H   6. G   7. E   8. F

IV 1. × difficult前加a   2. × are改为is   3. × one改为once

4. √   5. × piano前加the   6. × What改为How

7. √   8. × helps改为help

V 1. Do you like making friends? 你喜欢交朋友吗？

2. I started to play volleyball when I was very young. 我很小的时候就开始打排球了。

3. Can you cook at home? 你会在家做饭吗？

4. She has a round face. 她有一张圆脸。

5. Where do you do your favourite activities? 你在哪里做你最喜欢的活动？

6. What does he look like? 他长什么样？

7. We have known each other for many years. 我们已经认识很多年了。

8. I like reading books about animals. 我喜欢读关于动物的书。

VI 1. Yes, I like drawing. I often draw my own experiences and ideas on paper. 是的，我喜欢画画。我经常把自己的经历和想法画在纸上。

2. Sure, I often draw for fun. 当然，我经常为了好玩画画。

3. No, it's not boring. I like playing the guitar. I play the guitar every day. 不，不无聊。我喜欢弹吉他。我每天都弹吉他。

4. I think playing the guitar is more fun. I have participated in many performances and won some prizes. 我认为弹吉他更有趣。我参加过很多演出，获得过一些奖项。

5. Yes, I like playing table tennis. I often play table tennis in my spare time. 是的，我喜欢打乒乓球。我经常在业余时间打乒乓球。

6. Of course, I always feel good and relaxed after running. Running can make me keep fit. 当然，我在跑步后总是感觉很好、很放松。跑步可以使我保持健康。

7. Yes, swimming is fun. In summer, I often go swimming in the swimming pool with my friends. 是的，游泳很有趣。在夏天，我经常和朋友去游泳池游泳。

8. I don't think it matters whether we win or not. There is always winning or losing in a sports game. When we win, we are happy. When we lose, we can learn from our failure. 我认为输赢并不重要。体育比赛总是有输赢之分。当我们赢的时候，我们很高兴；当

我们失败时，我们可以从中吸取教训。

Week 6 每周一练

I 1. C   2. A   3. A   4. C   5. A   6. C

II 1. with   2. spend   3. are   4. has   5. plus   6. because

     7. listening   8. in   9. there   10. will

III 1. D   2. C   3. A   4. B   5. H   6. E   7. G   8. F

IV 1. × are改为is   2. × special前加a   3. × fast改为faster

     4. √   5. × had改为have   6. × Have改为Has

     7. × are改为do   8. √

V 1. Sam's hair is very short. 萨姆的头发很短。

2. All my friends have got laptops. 我所有的朋友都有笔记本电脑。

3. The end of this film is too sad. 这部电影的结局太悲伤了。

4. Teenagers don't email each other very often. 青少年之间不常发电子邮件。

5. What makes you most excited? 什么事最让你兴奋呢？

6. Who receives good wishes on special days? 谁会在特殊的日子里收到美好的祝愿呢？

7. She couldn't use a computer when she was three. 她三岁时还不会用电脑。

8. My phone can do lots of things. 我的手机可以做很多事情。

VI 1. No, I don't. I find it boring. I like watching talk shows on TV. 不，我不喜欢。我觉得新闻很无聊。我喜欢看电视上的脱口秀节目。

2. Yes, I like cartoons best. They are funny. Whenever I have time, I will watch cartoons. 是的，我最喜欢动画片。动画片很有趣。只要我有时间，我就会看动画片。

3. Sure, I love sports. I like watching sports matches on TV, especially football matches. 当然，我喜欢运动。我喜欢看电视上的体育比赛，尤其是足球比赛。

4. I like the cartoon *Tom and Jerry* the best. It's funny and entertaining. 我最喜欢卡通片《猫和老鼠》。它既有趣又令人愉快。

5. Yes, the Spring Festival is one of the traditional festivals in China. It's a time for family reunion. Before the festival, family members come back home. And usually, we have a big dinner on the New Year's Eve. 是的，我喜欢春节。春节是中国的传统节日之一。春节是家庭团聚的时刻。春节前夕，家人都会回家。通常，我们会在除夕吃一顿丰盛的

晚餐。

6. Of course, during the Dragon Boat Festival, we make rice dumplings, and we watch the dragon boat races. The dragon boat races are very exciting. 当然啦，我们在端午节期间包粽子、看龙舟赛。龙舟比赛是非常令人兴奋的。

7. Sure, New Year marks the beginning of a year. People usually make good wishes at the beginning of a year. 当然，新年标志着一年的开始。人们通常在新年伊始许下美好的愿望。

8. I like the Spring Festival best because I can get many red packets from my parents, grandparents, uncles and aunts during the festival. And then I can buy many things I like, such as stickers, books and toys. 我最喜欢春节，因为我可以从我的爸爸妈妈、爷爷奶奶、叔叔阿姨那里得到很多红包。然后我可以买很多我喜欢的东西，比如贴纸、书籍和玩具。

Week 7 每周一练

Ⅰ 1. A　　　2. B　　　3. C　　　4. A　　　5. A　　　6. B

Ⅱ 1. near　　　2. have　　　3. rooms　　　4. don't　　　5. go　　　6. things

7. your　　　8. took　　　9. time　　　10. cost

Ⅲ 1. C　　　2. D　　　3. B　　　4. A　　　5. H　　　6. G　　　7. E　　　8. F

Ⅳ 1. √　　　　　　2. × good前加a　　　　　3. × Does改为Do

4. × kind改为kinds　　　5. × Are改为Were　　　6. × wants改为want

7. √　　　　　　8. × going改为go

Ⅴ 1. Fast food is never healthy. 快餐从来都不健康。

2. We can walk to the park because it is not far. 我们可以步行去公园，因为它不远。

3. The museum is open on Sundays. 博物馆星期天开放。

4. The air in the countryside is very fresh. 乡下的空气很新鲜。

5. We don't need to wait for too long. 我们不需要等太久。

6. What is the best way to buy things cheaply? 买便宜东西的最好方法是什么？

7. I prefer to go to lots of different places. 我喜欢去很多不同的地方。

8. There is always a sale going on. 那里总有打折。

Ⅵ 1. Actually, I don't like eating at school because the food there is not good. 事实上，我不喜

欢在学校吃饭，因为学校的饭菜不好吃。

2. No, I don't think so. I seldom eat at the fast food restaurants. My mum told me that fast food such as burgers and potato chips is not good for health. 不，我不这么认为。我很少在快餐店吃饭。我妈妈告诉我，汉堡包和薯片等快餐对健康不好。

3. No, I like eating at home. My mum is good at cooking. I can have my favourite dishes. 不，我喜欢在家吃饭。我妈妈的厨艺很好。我可以吃到自己最喜欢的饭菜。

4. I prefer to eat at home, especially during traditional festivals. During festivals all of my relatives will come to my house and then we will have a big meal. 我更喜欢在家里吃饭，尤其是在传统节日期间。在节日期间，我所有的亲戚都会来我家，然后我们会吃一顿大餐。

5. Yes, I go there every weekend. It's fun to play badminton there. 是的，我每个周末都会去那里。在体育中心打羽毛球很有趣。

6. Yes, I like going to the museum. I can understand the world better on every visit. And most museums are free. 是的，我喜欢去博物馆。每去一次博物馆，我都能更好地了解这个世界。而且大多数博物馆是免费的。

7. Yes, the air there is fresh and there are lots of plants in the park. I often take a walk there after supper. 是的，公园里的空气很新鲜，公园里也有很多植物。我经常在晚饭后去公园散步。

8. I like the sports centre best. I can play in the sports centre. I can make friends there. I can enjoy the relaxing sports time, too. 我最喜欢体育中心。我可以在体育中心玩，我可以在那里交朋友，我还可以享受放松的运动时间。

Week 8 考试全流程模拟练习

Part 1-1

个人信息表			
Name	Li Ping	Age	11
Place	Chongqing		

1. My name is **Li Ping**. 我的名字叫李平。

2. **I'm fine**, thanks. 我很好，谢谢。

3. I'm from **Chongqing**. 我来自重庆。

4. I'm **eleven** years old. 我今年11岁。

Part 1-2

个人信息表		
	language 语言	**traffic 交通**
Candidate A	study English 学英语	mother drove me 妈妈开车送我
	for about six years 大约六年了	prefer to travel by train 更喜欢坐火车旅行 enjoy the natural scenery 欣赏自然风光
	Chinese 汉语 mother tongue 母语 speak Chinese very well 中文说得很好	
Candidate B	read English every morning 每天早晨读英语	walk to school 步行上学 close to the school 离学校很近
	a little bit hard 有点儿难 practice makes perfect 熟能生巧 confident 自信的	by airplane 乘飞机 see the blue sky and white clouds 看蓝天和白云 up close 近距离
		subway 地铁 convenient 便利的

5. I am **studying English** at school. 我在学校学英语。

6. I've studied it **for about six years**. 我已经学了六年英语。

7. Yes, I read English **every morning**. 是的，我每天早上读英语。

8. It's **a little bit hard** for me. My mum told me that **practice makes perfect**. I am **confident** that I can learn it well. 英语对我来说有点儿难。我妈妈告诉我熟能生巧。我相信我能够学好它。

9. My favourite language is **Chinese**. Chinese is my **mother tongue**, you know. I can **speak** Chinese **very well**. 我最喜欢的语言是汉语。你知道，中文是我的母语。我的中文说得很好。

10. I often **walk** to school. My home is **close to the school**. 我经常走路上学。我家离学校很近。

11. **Yes**, I do. I can **see the blue sky and white clouds up close**. 是的，我喜欢。我可以近距离

看到蓝天和白云。

12. My mother **drove** me here. 我妈妈开车送我来的。

13. I prefer to travel **by train**. I can **enjoy the natural scenery** along the way. 我更喜欢乘火车旅行。我可以欣赏沿途的自然风光。

14. Sure. My favourite public traffic is the **subway**. It is **convenient** to take the subway. 当然可以。我最喜欢的公共交通工具是地铁。乘地铁很方便。

Part 2

Phase 1

【考生对话】

		parrot 鹦鹉	kitten 小猫	rabbit 兔子	puppy 小狗	hamster 仓鼠
信息表						
Candidate A	喜欢/不喜欢		like 喜欢		dislike 不喜欢	
	理由		cute and independent 既可爱又独立		naughty and annoying 又淘气又烦人	
Candidate B	喜欢/不喜欢	like 喜欢		not exactly 不完全喜欢		dislike 不喜欢
	理由	the cleverest bird 最聪明的鸟		quiet, but smell 安静但有气味		bite 咬

A: Do you like parrots? 你喜欢鹦鹉吗？

B: Yes, I do. Parrots are **the cleverest bird** I have ever seen so far. Which animal do you like? 是的，我喜欢鹦鹉。鹦鹉是迄今为止我见过的最聪明的鸟。你喜欢哪种动物？

A: Actually, I like kittens very much. Kittens are **cute and independent**. Do you like rabbits? 事实上，我非常喜欢小猫。小猫既可爱又独立。你喜欢小兔子吗？

B: Not exactly. Rabbits are **quiet**, but they **smell**. What do you think of puppies? 不完全喜欢。兔子很安静，但它们有气味。你觉得小狗怎么样？

A: I don't like puppies. They are **naughty and annoying**. What about hamsters? 我不喜欢小狗。

它们又淘气又烦人。仓鼠呢?

B: Well, I don't like hamsters because they like to bite. 好吧，我不喜欢仓鼠，因为他们喜欢咬东西。

【考官问答】

信息表		parrot 鹦鹉	kitten 小猫	puppy 小狗	hamster 仓鼠
Examiner	问题		...best pet to keep? ……最好养的动物?	...annoying? ……烦人?	
Candidate A	回答		yes 是的	yes 是的	
	理由		cute and clean 既可爱又干净 independent 独立的	followed my grandma 跟着我奶奶 stay with their master 和主人待在一起	
Examiner	问题	...fun? ……有趣吗?			...cute? ……可爱吗?
Candidate B	回答	sure 当然			no 不
	理由	imitate human sounds 模仿人的声音 say hello 打招呼 interesting 有趣的			sharp teeth 锋利的牙齿 carry viruses 携带病毒 bad for our health 对我们健康有害

favourite animal 最喜欢的动物	
	parrots 鹦鹉
Candidate A / B	looks around 环顾四周 jumps 跳跃 say hello to visitors 向游客问好 lively and cute 活泼可爱

1. **No**, I don't like hamsters. They have **sharp teeth** that may hurt us. And they usually **carry**

viruses that are **bad for our health**. 不，我不喜欢仓鼠。仓鼠的牙齿很锋利，可能会伤害到我们。而且它们通常携带对我们健康有害的病毒。

2. **Yes**, I think so. My grandma used to keep a puppy. The puppy **followed my grandma** wherever she went. It seems that dogs like **staying with their master all the time**. 是的，我也觉得是。我奶奶以前养过一只小狗。无论奶奶到哪里，这只小狗都跟着她。狗狗们似乎喜欢一直黏着主人。

3. **Sure**. Parrots like to **imitate human sounds**. When you say hello to it, it will **say hello to you**. I find it **interesting** to keep a parrot at home. 当然啦。鹦鹉喜欢模仿人的声音。你跟它打招呼，它也会跟你打招呼。我觉得在家里养鹦鹉很有趣。

4. **Yes**, they are **cute and clean**. And they are **independent** and prefer to be alone in life. When a kitten is bored, it looks for toys to play with. 是的，小猫既可爱又干净。而且它们很独立，生活中喜欢独来独往。小猫在无聊时会找玩具玩。

5. I like parrots best. My grandpa keeps a parrot at home. The parrot sometimes **looks around,** sometimes **jumps**, and sometimes **say hello** to visitors. It is very **lively and cute**. 我最喜欢鹦鹉。我爷爷在家里养了一只鹦鹉。这只鹦鹉有时环顾四周，有时跳跃，有时向游客问好。它非常活泼可爱。

Phase 2

信息表			
Candidate A / B			
...go to the zoo or keep a pet at home? ……去动物园还是在家里养宠物?	选择	keep a pet at home 在家里养一只宠物	go to the zoo 去动物园
	理由	not a fan of the zoo 不喜欢动物园 very dangerous 非常危险 large animals 大型动物	see many animals 看到许多动物 such as monkeys and elephants 比如猴子和大象
...more popular, large animals or small animals? ……大动物还是小动物更受欢迎?	选择	small animals 小动物	large animals 大型动物
	理由	cute 可爱的 safe for humans 对于人类很安全	strong 强壮的 impressive 令人印象深刻的

6. I prefer to **keep a pet at home**. I'm **not really a fan of the zoo**. I think animals there are **very dangerous**, especially **large animals**. 我更喜欢在家里养宠物。我不太喜欢动物园。我认为那里的动物非常危险，尤其是大型动物。

/ I prefer to **go to the zoo**. I can **see many animals** in the zoo, **such as monkeys and elephants**. 我更喜欢去动物园。我可以在动物园看到许多动物，比如猴子和大象。

7. I think **small animals** are more popular because they are **cute and safe for humans**. 我认为小动物更受欢迎，因为对人类来说，它们既可爱又安全。

/ I think **large animals** are more popular because they are **strong** and **impressive**. 我认为大型动物更受欢迎，因为它们强壮，令人印象深刻。

附录

A2 Key不规则动词表

1. 改变元音字母

序号	变形规律	动词原形	过去式	中文释义
1	i变为a	begin [bɪˈgɪn]	began [bɪˈgæn]	开始
		drink [drɪŋk]	drank [dræŋk]	喝
		give [gɪv]	gave [geɪv]	给；交给；送给
		ring [rɪŋ]	rang [ræŋ]	响铃；按铃；给……打电话
		sing [sɪŋ]	sang [sæŋ]	唱歌
		sit [sɪt]	sat [sæt]	坐
		spit [spɪt]	spit [spɪt] /spat [spæt]	吐(唾沫、食物等)；怒斥
		swim [swɪm]	swam [swæm]	游泳
2	o变为a	become [bɪˈkʌm]	became [bɪˈkeɪm]	变得；成为
		come [kʌm]	came [keɪm]	来；出现
3	a变为o	wake [weɪk]	woke [wəʊk]	叫醒；醒来
4	i变为o	drive [draɪv]	drove [drəʊv]	驾驶
		ride [raɪd]	rode [rəʊd]	骑马；乘车
		shine [ʃaɪn]	shone [ʃɒn] /shined [ʃaɪnd]	闪光；闪耀
		win [wɪn]	won [wʌn]	赢得，获胜
		write [raɪt]	wrote [rəʊt]	写
5	e变为o	forget [fəˈget]	forgot [fəˈgɒt]	忘记
		get [get]	got [gɒt]	成为；获得；到达
6	o变为e	hold [həʊld]	held [held]	拿着，抓住；举行
7	ow/aw变为ew	blow [bləʊ]	blew [bluː]	吹；打击
		draw [drɔː]	drew [druː]	画；拉
		grow [grəʊ]	grew [gruː]	生长；种植

序号	变形规律	动词原形	过去式	中文释义
7	ow/aw变为ew	**kn**ow [nəʊ]	**kn**ew [njuː]	知道；了解
		throw [θrəʊ]	**thr**ew [θruː]	投，扔，抛
8	其他变化	**di**g [dɪg]	**du**g [dʌg]	挖
		fall [fɔːl]	**fe**ll [fel]	落下；跌倒
		hang [hæŋ]	**hu**ng [hʌŋ]	悬挂，吊
		run	**r**an	跑
9	省略相同字母中的一个	**cho**ose [tʃuːz]	**cho**se [tʃəʊz]	选择
		feed [fiːd]	**fe**d [fed]	喂养；进食
		meet [miːt]	**me**t [met]	遇见；集合；开会
		shoot [ʃuːt]	**sho**t [ʃɒt]	射击；射杀
10	去掉单词结尾的e	**bit**e [baɪt]	**bit** [bɪt]	咬
		hide [haɪd]	**hid** [rəʊt]	隐藏；躲避

（动词show除外，show—showed）

2. 改变辅音（元音+辅音）字母

序号	变形规律	动词原形	过去式	中文释义
1	省略两个相同字母中的一个，词尾加t	**feel** [fiːl]	**felt** [felt]	感觉
		keep [kiːp]	**kept** [kept]	保持；继续；养；饲养
		sleep [sliːp]	**slept** [slept]	睡觉
		sweep [swiːp]	**swept** [swept]	打扫
		smell [smel]	**smelt** [smelt]	闻
2	在动词原形后加一个辅音字母d或t	**burn** [bɜːn]	**burnt** [bɜːnt] / **burned** [bɜːnd]	燃烧；灼伤
		dream [driːm]	**dreamt** [dremt] / **dreamed** [driːmd]	做梦；梦想
		hear [hɪə(r)]	**heard** [hɜːd]	听见；听说
		learn [lɜːn]	**learnt** [lɜːnt] / **learned** ['lɜːnd]	学习；获悉；了解
		mean [miːn]	**meant** [ment]	意味着；意思是；打算

序号	变形规律	动词原形	过去式	中文释义
3	把动词原形的最后一个辅音字母d变为t	build [bɪld]	built [bɪlt]	建造
		send [send]	sent [sent]	发送；派遣；寄信
		spend [spend]	spent [spent]	度过；花费
4	k变为d	make [meɪk]	made [meɪd]	使，让；做，制造
5	y变为id	pay [peɪ]	paid [peɪd]	支付；给以报酬
		say [seɪ]	said [sed]	说，讲

3. 过去式为ought，aught

序号	变形规律	动词原形	过去式	中文释义
1	过去式为ought	bring [brɪŋ]	brought [brɔːt]	带来
		buy [baɪ]	bought [bɔːt]	购买
		think [θɪŋk]	thought [θɔːt]	想，思考；认为，以为
		seek [siːk]	sought [sɔːt]	寻找；搜寻
2	过去式为aught	catch [kætʃ]	caught [kɔːt]	抓住；赶上
		teach [tiːtʃ]	taught [tɔːt]	教学

4. 过去式和动词原形一样

变形规律	动词原形	过去式	中文释义
过去式和动词原形一样	bet [bet]	bet [bet]	打赌
	cost [kɒst]	cost [kɒst]	花费
	cut [kʌt]	cut [kʌt]	切，割
	hit [hɪt]	hit [hɪt]	打，打击
	hurt [hɜːt]	hurt [hɜːt]	伤害
	let [let]	let [let]	让，允许
	put [pʊt]	put [pʊt]	放；安置
	read [riːd]	read [red]	阅读；朗读
	shut [ʃʌt]	shut [ʃʌt]	关闭；关上
	spread [spred]	spread [spred]	展开；传播；散布

5. 情态动词的特殊变形

序号	动词原形	过去式	中文释义
1	can [kən]	could [kʊd]	能，会；可以；可能
2	may [meɪ]	might [maɪt]	可能，也许；可以
3	must [mʌst]	must [mʌst]	必须；一定
4	shall [ʃæl]	should [ʃʊd]	将要
5	will [wɪl]	would [wʊd]	将，将要

6. 其他不规则变形

序号	变形规律	动词原形	过去式	中文意思
1	ear变为ore	bear [beə(r)]	bore [bɔː(r)]	忍受
		wear [weə(r)]	wore [wɔː(r)]	穿（衣服、鞋），戴；损耗
2	eak变为oke	break [breɪk]	broke [brəʊk]	打破，破碎；损坏
		speak [spiːk]	spoke [spəʊk]	讲话；发言；讲述
3	ell变为old	sell [sel]	sold [səʊld]	出售；转让；推销
		tell [tel]	told [təʊld]	告诉；讲述
4	ake变为ook	shake [ʃeɪk]	shook [ʃʊk]	摇动；摇头；握手
		take [teɪk]	took [tʊk]	拿；采取；花费
5	无规律变化	eat [iːt]	ate [eɪt]	吃
		find [faɪnd]	found [faʊnd]	找到；发现
		go [gəʊ]	went [went]	去，走
		have [həv]	had [hæd]	有；做；进行；从事
		leave [liːv]	left [left]	离开；留下
		lie [laɪ]	lay [leɪ]（躺）lied [laɪd]（说谎）	说谎；躺
		lose [luːz]	lost [lɒst]	丢失；丧失；被打败
		see [siː]	saw [sɔː]	看见，看出；观看
		stand [stænd]	stood [stʊd]	站立；起立
		steal [stiːl]	stole [stəʊl]	偷，窃取

国际音标和单词的发音

国际音标（International Phonetic Alphabet），简称IPA，由国际语音协会的语言学家编制。它由20个元音和28个辅音组成，共48个音标。

IPA国际音标		发音实例			
元音	短元音 （7个）	[ɪ]	big	[ɒ]	want
		[e]	next	[ʊ]	put
		[æ]	happy	[ə]	about
		[ʌ]	colour		
	长元音 （5个）	[i:]	he	[u:]	rule
		[ɑ:]	last	[ɜ:]	bird
		[ɔ:]	or		
	双元音 （8个）	[eɪ]	make	[eə]	hair
		[aɪ]	bike	[uə]	actual
		[ɔɪ]	toy	[əʊ]	home
		[ɪə]	idea	[aʊ]	now
辅音	清辅音 （8个）	[p]	pen	[θ]	thing
		[t]	party	[s]	so
		[k]	class	[ʃ]	wish
		[f]	feel	[h]	hot
	浊辅音 （14个）	[b]	buy	[m]	must
		[d]	day	[n]	nice
		[g]	go	[ŋ]	sing
		[v]	visit	[l]	leave
		[ð]	this	[r]	read
		[z]	easy	[j]	youth
		[ʒ]	leisure	[w]	win
	鼻辅音 （3个）	[m]	many	[n]	neck
		[ŋ]	thing		
	半元音（2个）	[w]	with	[j]	yes
	舌侧音（1个）	[l]	lab		

小马外语